The Virgin Gardener

BLOOMSBURY

Contents

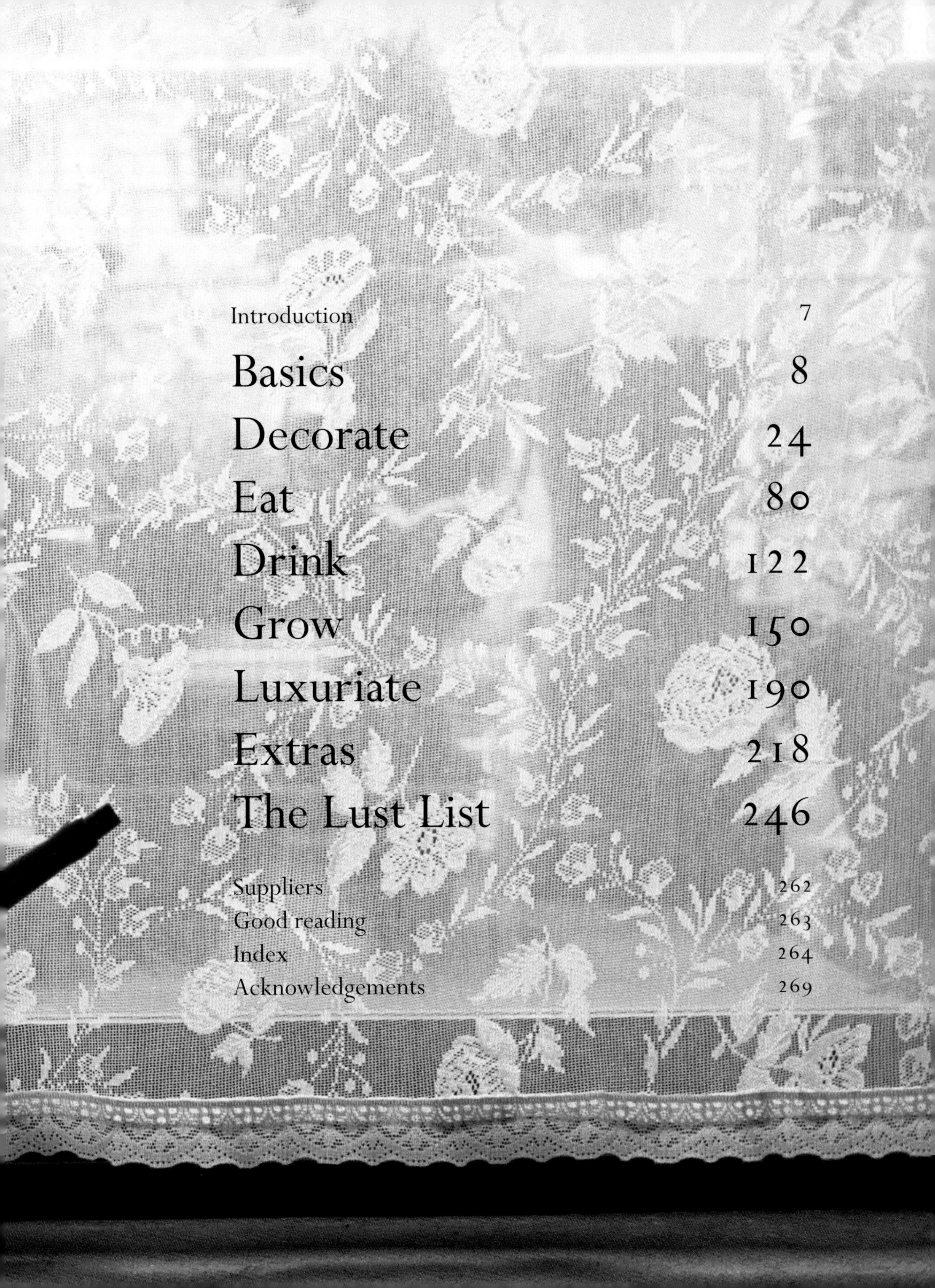

Introduction

In my twenties the Outside was what I ventured through on my way somewhere, usually to a party after dark. I rarely frequented green spaces, knew nothing about plants and had no interest whatsoever in gardening. A few years ago my mother gave me a packet of seeds and, to alleviate the boredom of my office job, I planted them. They sprouted. I resigned from my job, enrolled on a horticultural course at the Chelsea Physic Garden in London, and was instantly and irretrievably hooked on gardening.

Everyone around me on the course had a garden of some description. I lived in a London flat with a tiny balcony and an entrance yard with some steps. I felt at such a disadvantage that for a while I seriously considered moving and finding somewhere with outside space so that I could create the gardens I was learning about and dreaming of: cool, damp, ferny glades; walkways heaving with scented roses; luscious banks of white gladioli, their centres blotched with deep maroon; and hidden rockeries with fuzzy, moss-covered stones. Then I began to read about what I'd have to do in order to have these things, and initially the jargon and the sheer volume of information overwhelmed me.

But gradually I learned the basic principles of working with plants successfully and discovered a way of gardening that suited me and the circumstances in which I live. Without throwing out my high heels or trying to turn the pavement into an allotment, I've grown the gardens of my dreams. I've recreated those banks of scented gladioli in tiered pots on my balcony. My rosy fix is a clandestine teaspoon of sticky rosehip syrup. I sleep beneath ferny fronds and I have pots of mossy hummocks indoors and out. For me, the challenge is to create abundance despite being space-, time- and cash-poor.

This is essentially a plant 'cookbook' of easy and accessible projects for virgin gardeners. The projects are in recipe form – bait that would have hooked me as a beginner – and they are all easy, inexpensive and perfect for virgins: the sort of ideas that would have seduced me into an afternoon with plants and rendered the garnering of knowledge a serendipitous by-product. There are also small sections containing all the useful information that I wished I had to hand when I began, and a list of some of the plants that have stolen my heart in the few short years I have been noticing these things.

If you've never done it before, or have been disappointed in the past, these ideas will show you how to get intimate with plants and sex up your living space – indoors or out – without the complicated jargon and off-putting diagrams. You don't have to own a garden, you don't have to get dirty and it won't take up all your time. This book will replace the fear of failure with a sense of fun, so take a deep breath and jump into the flowerbed.

Basics

Most gardeners learn the basics by trial and error and through watching others. Knowledge acquired in this way becomes engrained very fast – and consequently information that is baffling to the virgin seems too obvious to experienced gardeners to be worth relating. The upshot is that a whole tranche of explanation – the stuff virgins want to know but may be too scared to ask – gets left out of the conversation.

Here are the things I wanted to know when I began, set out in a way I would have understood. There is no a secret algorithm that will guarantee success, but these simple rules of thumb will set you off in the right direction.

How to grow plants

To grow plants successfully, you have to make them feel at home and give them what they need. Here's how:

1. Find out where they come from, by using either the internet or a plant A–Z. When you've discovered a plant's place of origin (e.g. southern China) and habitat (e.g. mountain regions), try to replicate that environment as far as possible. Even if you don't know anything about mountain regions in southern China, this information will imprint an image on your mind of where this particular plant likes to be, and that will be hugely helpful as you grow it, because without necessarily being aware of it you will instinctively understand that it won't be very happy next to the boggy pond at the bottom of your garden.

2. Find out the hardiness of the plant, again by looking it up, or by asking the person who's selling it. Any plant is hardy in its natural environment – that is, able to survive outside all the year round – but may not be able to endure the climatic conditions, like frost, elsewhere. A plant's hardiness rating is nothing more than a shorthand way of establishing the lowest temperature that a plant can withstand without keeling over and dying. You already have an idea of the plant's hardiness when you find out where it comes from, but the good people at the Royal Horticultural Society (RHS) have simplified the business for us, using symbols as follows:

SYMBOL	LOWEST TEMPERATURE PLANT CAN WITHSTAND	WHAT IT BASICALLY MEANS
***	−15°C	**Fully hardy** – i.e. fine outside all year round.
**	−5°C	**Frost hardy** – i.e. fine outside in warmer areas or sheltered places; can withstand the odd frost but nothing prolonged.
*	0°C	**Half hardy** – i.e. can't survive outside in winter
^*	5°C	**Frost-tender** – i.e. probably a houseplant; needs to be kept reasonably warm all year round.

Please note that it's really important not to get hung up on the issue of hardiness – and a plant's rating should only be used as a guide.

3. Supply the plant with the following:
Water   Light   Nutrients

In fact, even if you don't do 1 and 2, just do this, and your plant will grow.

Definitions

If you know which category or sub-category a plant belongs to, it's much easier to look after it properly because you'll know what behaviour to expect from it. Here is the lowdown:

TREES Long lived and woody, deciduous (drops its leaves in autumn) or evergreen. Usually notable for having a trunk, but sometimes has more than one … I won't go on – you know what a tree is.

SHRUBS Woody stemmed, deciduous or evergreen, like a tree, but branching from lower down – and, of course, they're smaller. As with everything in gardening, there are some grey areas. Some large shrubs are also small trees, and vice versa. There are also some plants that are only partially woody, which people call subshrubs, and there are some that die back every year, and are therefore treated as perennials (see below).

CLIMBERS Plants that grow upwards over a support (including other plants) using a variety of different methods such as clinging, twining or scrambling around. They are amazing and glorious to watch as they grow, as well as being hugely valuable plants, particularly in a small space, as they add a vertical dimension.

PERENNIALS Plants that live for more than two years and flower every year once they're mature. They die down after flowering and come up again in spring (although, yet again, there are exceptions to this, as some are evergreen or semi-evergreen). If you've never gardened before, and if you're anything like me, you will come to value perennials after you have had a mad passionate love affair with annuals (see below), showstoppers though they are. Gardening with a perennial is like meeting someone reliable and kind and beautiful who you can see yourself settling down with, rather than having a wild, flash-in-the-pan romance that ends all too soon.

TENDER PERENNIALS Plants from warmer climes that won't survive our winter, so usually we grow them from seed every year (like annuals, below); or you can bring them indoors over winter if you're lucky enough to have a conservatory or somewhere light and frost-free.

ANNUALS Plants that grow from seed, set seed and die all in the space of one year. Because they don't have a lot of time, they grow fast, and most have incredible colour and scent so as to attract as much attention to themselves as possible from pollinators (like bees). These plants can be bought in flower but are so easy to grow from seed that most people don't waste their money.

BIENNIALS	Just like annuals, but with a two-year life cycle. Generally they produce leaves in the first year and flowers the next.
ALPINES AND ROCK PLANTS	A group of plants from mountainous areas all over the world: all grow above the tree line and, as you can imagine, they like rocky places. They're mostly tiny (because it would be a waste of energy to be a big plant in such inhospitable conditions). They need a degree of special care in terms of where they are kept, but they are utterly beautiful and totally worth it.
BULBOUS PLANTS	This term usually describes any plant that has a food storage organ underground, and therefore includes true bulbs, corms, tubers and rhizomes. Bulbous plants usually have a 'dormant' period (only dormant to us) underground, during which they replenish this organ and get ready to come up again and delight us.
ORCHIDS	Amazing, highly specialised perennials which have developed extraordinary ways of surviving. They mostly come from tropical rainforests, although we have wonderful native orchids of our own which are to be treasured. The orchids with which we are most familiar are specially cultivated hybrids and grown indoors. They are expensive, and therefore it is worth knowing something about how to grow them well; in fact it's easy to get them flowering year after year (see page 167).
BROMELIADS	Mainly rainforest plants, and therefore suitable as houseplants only if the air is kept moist enough. Commonly sold in garden centres and weirdly decorative.
CACTI AND SUCCULENTS	Brilliant plants to have, because they're specially adapted to survive long periods of drought, so very hard to kill. Because they're used to dry air they do really well in our houses, too.
PALMS AND CYCADS	Evergreen trees or shrubs from tropical and subtropical areas that are used in every office in the country … and if they can survive that they deserve our unbridled respect.
FERNS	I am in love with this group of primitive plants. Evergreen or deciduous, they come in a variety of forms and hardinesses, which means that they are useful as well as beautiful.
AQUATIC PLANTS	These plants grow in or under or around water, and are subdivided into various different categories, depending on how deep they like to be.

Buying plants

Small specialist nurseries are brilliant: even if you don't buy from them,
they are always ready to help, as most of them are completely nutty about
their subject. The main reason I use them, though, is that I can be relatively
certain that the plant I'm buying has been propagated on site – rather than in
another country – by an expert who really cares about what he or she is
doing. In addition, I get to have a dialogue with the grower, which is worth
ten times what I pay for the plant. Most of these places sell by mail order.

This is not in any way to persuade you to avoid large garden centres,
which are an equally valuable resource, particularly when it comes to value
for money and stocking most of the more popular varieties we want in our
gardens. They also often have fabulously knowledgeable staff.

We all think we know how to pick the apple or strawberry that's likely to
taste best – it's the one that looks nicest to us, whether that means shiny,
flawless skin, vibrant colour, good shape, firm texture or enticing smell.
Sometimes, though, the reddest apple can yield an awful, woolly, tasteless
mouthful. Happily, this is not true of plants, so let your instincts guide you.
The only caveat to this is that with plants bushiness is always a better bet than
height: the tallest is not necessarily the best.

Essential stuff

I have the following things:

SECATEURS Even if your contact with plants extends only to putting flowers in a vase, it's worth investing in a good pair of secateurs. Cheap ones really are a false economy. I have a pair made by Felco, who also make other good garden tools. You can get a pair of Felcos in a size to suit your hands, and in left-handed versions. Mine are size 8. All Felcos have bright red handles, which makes them easy to spot in the undergrowth.

HAND TROWEL If you don't already have one knocking around (I seemed – inexplicably – to have amassed a vast selection of trowels before I even started gardening), you'll need to get a hand trowel. Stainless steel is best, with a wooden handle that feels comfortable in your hand.

GLOVES Under-the-fingernail dirt is a passion-killer, so if I'm going to be doing a lot of work with soil I sometimes use gloves. Ordinary gardening gloves are useless because you can't feel anything in them, and I just end up taking them off. I use something called Foxgloves, which are stretchy, soft and go in the washing machine. I also have a large collection of nail polishes, which cover a multitude of sins.

WATERING CANS You can never have too many of these. I keep full watering cans in every area of my space. Make sure yours has a rose (an attachment with little holes) so the water comes out gently, like rain.

SQUIRTER Some plants, like ferns, orchids and moss, love to be sprayed with a fine mist of water, which mimics the damp conditions they enjoy in their natural habitats. This is particularly important indoors, where the air is extremely dry, even without the central heating on. You can buy plastic squirty bottles in any hardware or DIY store. Fill them with water and keep them near any plants that enjoy a humid atmosphere, so that you can mist them whenever you pass by.

POTS You can never have too many. It's best to buy pots for specific plants rather than lots in one go. Terracotta are cheap and look great. Make sure they are frost-proof and have holes in the bottom.

POT SAUCERS Every time you buy a pot, get a saucer to go with it. It may seem a boring thing to spend money on, but it will improve your life immeasurably (see page 225).

LARGE PLASTIC TRAYS For holding pots inside and outside, and wonderful for when you go on holiday, as you can group your plants together on them and put water in the bottom.

TUB TRUG	A plastic tub with handles, excellent for mixing compost in, carrying things around in and keeping things clean.
POTTING TRAY	A plastic tray with a back and sides that you put on a table. It keeps all your mess in one place – brilliant for when you are sowing seeds.
SEED TRAYS	For sowing seeds. Seed trays often come with lids, so you can use one as a propagator (see below). I also use seed trays for sowing salad leaves in.
PROPAGATOR	When I bought my propagator, the little voice inside my head (the same one that orders me never to eat sticky toffee pudding) told me it would end up in a cupboard full of things I never use. We all have a cupboard like this; mine contains, amongst other things, a potato ricer, some retro kitchen scales and three coffee grinders. I thanked the voice for pointing this out and bought the thing anyway. It transformed my plant world.

Most seeds like a warm, humid environment in which to germinate and begin their lives as plants. The warmth is an indication that it's safe to come out, and the humidity inhibits the rate at which the leaves of the young plant lose water (a process known as transpiration). This means that the roots can put all their energy into growing down, rather than transporting water. If you are interested in growing plants, a propagator will improve and enhance your life massively. There are two types you can get:

1. **Simple propagator** This is just a tray with a lid on it. You can get them to fit on your windowsill.
2. **Heated propagator** This is the thing to get when you've been working with seeds for a little while and have decided you like it. You plug it in and the tray heats up to the optimum level for germinating most seeds. Some have a dial so that you can fiddle about with the temperature, but mine doesn't. It has a lid, just as the simple propagators do, with vents in it to increase airflow if you want.

Propagators are like most other products: you can find very expensive swanky ones and dirt-cheap ones, and there are good ones and bad ones at both ends of this scale. Whichever you choose, do get one; if you never use it, there is always eBay.

WELLIES	I use wellies in winter and summer, often putting them on to water in the morning and finding myself still wearing them when I turn up to meet friends in the evening.
NOTEBOOK	Absolutely essential, so that I can remember what I've done. It's really good to have a small book handy for the following reasons:

※ Whenever you see something delightful, you can write down the name of it.

※ When you see a plant you love but you don't know the name of it, you can put a piece of it inside and identify it later. This is much better than a photograph.

※ You can kneel on it to sniff things when the ground is soggy.

Always choose a hardback book (I have one of those Moleskine ones with an elastic band, which is very useful for keeping things inside), and I use a pencil, because pencils don't stop working in the rain. I also keep some sticky labels in the back of the book, so I can stick bits of foliage to the pages.

BOOKS   There are certain books I go back to again and again (they are covered in dirt). I have marked them with a flower on page 263.

STUFF FOR MY PLANTS   See Compost in bags (page 20) and Feeding (page 229).

Compost in bags

If you have a garden or allotment, then you have soil to plant in. If you don't, you'll be buying bags of compost and the choice is troubling. Here's what it all means:

JOHN INNES COMPOST   John Innes was an amateur gardener who kindly bequeathed some cash to set up an institute in East Anglia. The people there developed a recipe for producing a standard growing medium that was suitable for most plants. It is a mixture of the following:

Loam Soil made of equal amounts of sand, silt and clay, which contains lots of nutrients.
Peat Allows air in and holds water.
Sand Provides drainage.

The recipe has changed over the years because of the reduced availability of loam. Companies produce John Innes compost in different strengths: John Innes No. 1, No. 2 and No. 3. The higher the number, the more nutrients the compost contains. No. 1 is used for seeds, which need little food, No. 2 for growing on young plants, and No. 3 for established plants.

In practice, this is all pretty tedious, not least because the loam in John Innes compost makes the bags horribly heavy to carry. However, John Innes is the compost to use for long-term plantings, as it holds water well and provides nutrients.

PEAT   Peat bogs are being pillaged, so although it's a fabulous compost constituent, using it in any quantity spoils my enjoyment. There are plenty of good composts around that are peat-free – the trick is to know which are the best.

MULTI-PURPOSE COMPOST   This is loam-free, which makes it much lighter, and suitable for temporary displays. It can be mixed with John Innes (which is what I do) for permanent plantings. All the companies who make multi-purpose have a different recipe: some are OK and others are utterly dire. Choosing a good multi-purpose compost can make the difference between loving or hating gardening, so it's really worth getting the right one. This means not just picking up any old bag of multi-purpose (the large DIY stores' branded products are some of the worst). Trials are done on a regular basis and the best peat-free one by far at the time of writing is one called 'multi-purpose peat-free compost', made by a company called New Horizon. The bag is bright green with vibrant orange flowers emblazoned across it. Another one called 'Westland peat-free multi-purpose compost with added John Innes' comes a very close second.

There are also composts that contain extra nutrients and water-retaining granules – the list is endless and confusing. I can't bear having all those bags hanging around and working out which to use for what, so I simplify things by having the following on the go:

New Horizon multi-purpose, which I use for practically everything.
John Innes No. 2, which I mix with it for longer-term plantings.

OTHER
INGREDIENTS

Horticultural grit for mixing with multi-purpose compost in order to sow seeds (if I don't have any seed compost to hand), and for mixing into compost to add drainage.

Seed compost for raising seeds in (multi-purpose mixed with grit is fine, but it often has big 'bits' in it, and seeds prefer something finer).

Pea gravel mulch for putting on top of pots to retain moisture and to discourage small animals from digging around.

A small bag of sand for planting bulbs.

Slow-release fertiliser granules to add to compost (see page 229).

Water-retaining granules or gel for pots and hanging baskets.

AND MORE

Ericaceous compost, which I buy if I want to grow acid-loving plants, such as blueberries.

Cactus compost and orchid compost, which I buy when needed, which is not often.

Get people to deliver this stuff wherever possible – it's heavy.

And before you begin ...

There has never been a single plant in the history of the world that didn't grow because it was scared it might die. Humans do this sort of thing all the time – not doing things because there's a chance it might all go wrong. Ninety-nine per cent of success in gardening depends on a certain attitude, and on knowing some very basic things about plants. Below is a list of principles that helped me when I began. Most of them pander to my own emotional needs. Plants don't have these issues and are therefore much simpler to look after than humans.

1. There is no magic in growing plants – just things we don't know yet.

2. 'Green fingers' do not exist. I have murdered a multitude of plants (and still do) not because I lack some kind of mystical ability but because I didn't follow some really basic principles, the most important of which is the employment of common sense.

3. Plants want to grow – that is their thing. They do not have inhibitions or whimsical insecurities. They are not callous or contrary. Unlike us, they do not suffer from bad hair days or sulkiness. All they care about is survival and sex.

4. Experimentation is essential if you're going to learn anything. Just because it didn't work the first time it doesn't mean you're cursed. Learn why it went wrong, and try again.

5. Creating an outdoor (or indoor) space using plants is possible in any situation. You do not have to be a) wealthy b) talented c) old and grey and cardigan-clad or d) young and strong and good at DIY.

6. You do not need to have a garden to have plants.

7. You can grow plants and do everything else; it won't take up all your time (unless you want it to).

8. Plants can enhance any area of your life – please yourself.

9. Growing stuff makes you more attractive; plants are all about living, and that is infectious.

Decorate

For me, this is where it all began: having plants or flowers in sight or within arm's length is my favourite way of pleasing myself. I am scarily capricious when it comes to my surroundings, frequently waking up with a passionate yearning for something different. A change of scene creates a change of mood, and you can do this with plants. There is no space in the world that isn't transformed by their presence.

Plants have become props on the stage-set of my life. One week I am surrounded by the austere beauty of stone and ferns; the next, I wade around in a sea of lavender; and then one day, suddenly and without warning, only roses will do.

Start decorating with plants and you enter a whole new dimension in terms of mood (when has a new piece of furniture ever smelled like the heady waxiness of a lily in full bloom?). On top of this, a plant is a growing thing, changing all the time, and giving out oxygen as it does so.

The following pages are all things that I do with plants to create atmosphere and change my scene. They require minimal time, effort and money and are intended as suggestions only, for your own modifications and whims. And of course, nothing could be more satisfying than sexing up your space and showing it off to your friends to produce pleasure and jealousy in equal measure; we are only human, after all.

Thyme

I use thyme for decorating more than I use it for food, principally because I regard my many pots as a collection rather than a crop – one man's thyme is another man's Swarovski teddy bear, but thyme doesn't need dusting. Seriously, though, this is a lovely way of bringing the outside in. Thymes are slow growing, fabulously aromatic and wonderfully tactile, which makes them great container candidates (although you can, of course, grow them in a sunny, well-drained site in the ground). I have them in lots and lots of pots, in different shapes and sizes and colours; I can't be precious about making sure everything is uniform, as I buy little pots of thyme whenever I happen to spy a species I don't yet have – and that is alarmingly often.

THE LOWDOWN
Most species of thyme (*Thymus*) come from the Mediterranean, which means that they like things dry and sunny and gritty, rather than cold and wet. They are evergreen hardy perennials, which means that your pot of thyme will always be a pot of thyme, and you can pick it fresh, little and often, throughout the year.

THYMING
Buy thyme whenever you see it, but re-pot it in spring.

YOU WILL NEED
Pots of thyme Available from garden centres or nurseries.
Multi-purpose compost
Horticultural grit
Pots to plant them in Terracotta is best, and slightly larger than the pots the thyme is sold in.
A sunny site

METHOD
Mix your compost with one-third grit (this makes it free-draining) and plant your thymes, giving each one its own pot. Place your plants in the sunniest possible site you have. For me this means a south-facing windowsill or the outermost edge of my balcony. The more sun they get, the more aromatic oil is produced and the better they will smell.

Thyme is staggeringly low maintenance – I water it very sparingly in summer (and by that I mean once every four to five days, depending on the weather – you want the pot to remain pretty dry but not parched) and hardly at all in winter (cold is fine, but cold and damp is not).

Different thymes have different growth habits, so let the creeping ones creep and the trailing ones trail, picking bits off them regularly to keep them producing new leaves at the bottom and to prevent them from becoming 'woody' and sparse.

The ones that grow in mounds can be kept nice and hummocky if you indulge in the mindless activity of trimming them after flowering to create cloud-like, thymey tuffets.

***Thymus caespititius* (sometimes called *T. azoricus*)** Low-growing with bright green leaves and pale pink flowers in summer. Comes from Portugal.

***T.* × *citriodorus* (lemon thyme)** A man-made cross that produces leaves with a strong lemony scent. It comes in loads of varieties, all with different-coloured leaves. I like 'Bertram Anderson', which has grey-green leaves shot through with yellow. 'Silver Queen' is another beauty, with grey-silver variegated leaves.

***T. ericoides* 'Fragrantissimus' (orange-scented thyme)** Use this when cooking duck – yum.

***T. doerfleri* 'Bressingham'** Has grey-green leaves and candy-floss pink flowers in summer. Comes from Albania.

***T. herba-barona* (caraway thyme)** Has tiny dark green leaves with a caraway scent. Comes from Sardinia and Corsica.

***T. pulegioides* (broad-leaved thyme)** Low-growing with pink flowers in late spring and early summer. Very aromatic. Comes from Europe.

T. serpyllum Mat-forming, and comes in many varieties. I love 'Snowdrift', which has loads of white flowers in summer.

***T. vulgaris* (common thyme)** Bog-standard, no-messing-about thyme – the thyme you probably know. It can be found growing wild from the western Med to southern Italy. There is a very pretty form of it called 'Silver Posie', which has lilac flowers in summer and grey-variegated leaves.

Pinks for petals

A few gloriously sweet-smelling pinks in a pot is one of the nicest things a person can give him or herself, so here's the recipe for a simple pot of pinks.

THE LOWDOWN
Pinks come from the genus *Dianthus*, a group of plants that also includes carnations and other pinks which are not strictly pinks but are known as such. Hundreds of thousands of different cultivars have been bred by gardeners who get utterly obsessed with them – no doubt there are pink chatrooms all over the web. All that's important to me is that most of them are extremely good-looking evergreen, hardy perennials – making them permanent fixtures rather than plants that disappear and get forgotten about over winter – and that some of them smell deeply, astonishingly good.

By the way, the name 'pink' has nothing to do with colour (although most of them are pink) but comes from the serrated petals, which look as if they've been cut with pinking shears. *Dianthus* are mountain and meadow plants, and that means they like 'poor' soil.

TIMING
Spring to summer.

YOU WILL NEED
A *Dianthus* that you love My favourites right now are *D.* 'Mrs Sinkins', which is white, *D.* 'Doris', which is pink with a scarlet centre, *D.* 'Moulin Rouge', which is shocking pink with white petal tips, and *D.* 'Gran's Favourite', which is white with pink stripes. All are scented and widely available. You can buy them as mature plants in bud, or as rooted cuttings, which are a bit cheaper but may not flower until the next year.
A pot fit for it Choose one that is the same size or larger than the pot the plant's in. A window box is also a good idea, and of course you can plant pinks in the ground, as long as your soil is free draining (if not, add plenty of grit).
Multi-purpose compost mixed with lots of horticultural grit.
A sunny site

METHOD
Fill your pot (if you are using one) with compost and plant your pinks, taking care not to cover the bottom leaves with any soil (keep them at the same level they were in their plastic pots). Water them in well. Your pinks should flower from May to November, as long as you deadhead them (see page 231 for deadheading). They don't need anything else.

AND MORE
The petals are edible – they're exquisite in salads and on puddings – as long as you remove the white 'heel' that comes off with them (this part tastes bitter). The prettiest, most Martha Stewarty thing of all is to crystallise them by painting them with stiffly whisked egg white, dusting them with granulated sugar and allowing them to dry.

Ceropegia on a sconce

This is really an extension of a decorating trick I absorbed from my mother, who often places one beautiful thing on its own in an unexpected place with the result that it becomes art. This usually takes the form of something like a polished apple on the corner of a mantelpiece.

Being the sort of person who lurks in plant nurseries, I frequently come home with a tiny pot of something I couldn't resist and need somewhere to put it so that I can gloat over it for a few days while I find it a home. For this purpose I started putting sconces on the walls to act as little altars for my treasures, and I realised that displaying plants this way was far more fun, and much cheaper, than buying art. Then I discovered ceropegia, which can live permanently indoors with hardly any care and which clothe my white walls oh-so-tastefully with pale blue-grey trailing hearts.

THE LOWDOWN — *Ceropegia linearis* subsp. *woodii*, or 'Hearts on a string', can be found in most good garden centres and nurseries in the indoor plant section. It's an evergreen succulent, comes from the Eastern Cape and is utterly undemanding, doing nothing but looking beautiful all winter long and coming alive in spring, when it puts out new, grey-green shoots and tiny, weird pinkish flowers. The trailing stems can grow up to 1m long.

TIMING — Any time.

YOU WILL NEED — **Pots of *Ceropegia linearis* subsp. *woodii***
Prettier pots to put them in (Optional.)
Sconces, a mantelpiece or a shelf You can find sconces in flea markets and antique shops, but those 'magic' shelves that you can screw into the wall and look as if they're floating would do just as well.

METHOD — You can leave each ceropegia in its plastic pot and hide it inside something prettier, and simply place the whole thing on your sconce or shelf to sit there and look gorgeous. Water it once a week from spring to autumn, giving it a good soak in the sink each time. Don't water it at all between autumn and spring.

AND MORE — If you want more plants for nothing, wait until each little tuber has at least two stems coming out of it and carefully dig one out of the pot. It's best to do this before all the trailing stems have had a chance to muddle themselves up; otherwise it's like separating strings of beads. Fill a small pot (about 8cm in diameter) with cactus compost up to 1cm from the rim, and place the tuber so that the roots are buried in the compost and the tuber is sitting on top; then fill the remaining space with horticultural grit or fine gravel (this will prevent the tuber from rotting). If you water sparingly and are kind, new shoots should appear in a fortnight or so.

Twiggy grids

If, as in my flat, vases are heavily outnumbered by bowls, here is an easy way to make use of the latter for displaying blooms. I find this particularly useful when an arrangement in an ordinary vase begins to look tired. If you just cut off the flowers on short stalks and get rid of the foliage, you get something that looks completely fresh (and in many cases a lot nicer). Twiggy grids are a great way to display these blooms, and also supermarket or garage-type flowers, which look ridiculous and frankly sad on long stems.

TIMING
Any time.

YOU WILL NEED
Flowers on short stalks See above.
A collection of twigs These need to be straightish and roughly the same thickness. Notice how discerning dogs are when choosing a suitable stick and learn from them.
Secateurs
Some garden twine Choose natural, soft and malleable twine, not any old wiry, springy stuff (Nutscene is good). By the way, a big ball of nice string is one of the best presents you can give anyone.

METHOD
Cut all your twigs the same length. If you have a particular bowl in mind, make sure that the twigs are slightly longer than its diameter. Now get someone to hold two sticks together at right angles so that they touch a couple of centimetres shy of their ends, one atop the other, and tie them tightly together with the twine, with a knot. Do the same with another two sticks to create a square.

Keep adding sticks, tying their ends to this framework at regular intervals: one layer going one way, so that it looks like a ladder, and the next layer at right angles, so that you have a grid.

Now finish your twiggy grid off by snipping the ends of the string very close to the knots so that they're neat.

Rest the grid on top of the bowl and poke a bloom (or blooms) through each hole, making sure their stems are in the water. Remember that your handiwork is very much part of the whole thing and not supposed to be hidden.

AND MORE
Another way of doing this sort of thing if you're pushed for time is to wedge a layer of chicken wire inside a bowl. You achieve a similar effect, but working with chicken wire is a life-sapping experience and not really to be recommended.

A wall of ferns

An evergreen hardy fern is the virgin's ultimate plant. I use ferns everywhere, particularly to lush up my home and as ground cover for difficult areas of outdoor space. One fern in a pot is by turns calming, majestic and mysterious, but you can create anything from quiet formality to something resembling Mandalay, depending on how and in what numbers you use them. My all-time favourite table decoration is a big urn filled with lots of ferns, but you can also use ferns to clothe a whole wall.

THE LOWDOWN

The point about ferns is that they are really, really old. Fossils of ferns have been found dating back nearly 400 million years – that's before the flowering plants that we are familiar with existed. Because they have no flowers to produce seeds, ferns reproduce by using minuscule spores, contained in those spots that are visible on the undersides of some of the foliage. When you think that the dinosaurs all thundered through great swathes of this stuff, you get how successful this system is.

All ferns grow best in semi- or full shade, and many grow very well in cracks on stone walls. Because not everyone has a stone wall, but many may have an ordinary one that's shady (and I mean indoors or out), I've included the following project as a great way of mimicking this look. Of course, you can put any potted plant up on a wall using this method, but most need more light than ferns, which is why you should save any wall space that gets some natural light, and use ferns to cover dark spaces where nothing else will grow.

TIMING

Any time.

YOU WILL NEED

Ferns These are sold all year round. You can either get lots of small ones from the local garden centre or nursery (and by small, I mean ferns that don't grow more than 30–45cm tall), or really give yourself a treat and get a catalogue from the specialist on page 262 and choose from hundreds of precious little gems. Make sure every single one you buy is different, with a mixture of evergreen and deciduous. Bear in mind that some ferns are tender, so must be either grown indoors or at least brought indoors for the winter. See my favourites opposite.

A trellis panel with some hooks I use this method because it means that I can move my pots around easily, but you can get the same effect without a trellis by fixing nails or hooks securely into the wall.

Some secure plant hangers See Suppliers, page 262. These are the easiest and best way I have found of hanging pots on walls. Alternatively you could go out and find a few of those pots which are flat on one side and have a hole so that you can hook them up on a wall.

Pots A pot measuring 20cm in diameter is perfect for a 45cm-high fern.

Compost Most ferns like a growing medium rich in humus, and you can provide this by making leafmould (see page 162) and mixing it with soil. Otherwise ordinary multi-purpose will do.

Get someone to do all the DIY stuff if you hate doing it yourself (although I have to tell you that there is very little in life that comes close to the satisfaction derived from wielding a power drill). Either fix nails securely into the wall or hang S-bend hooks from the trellis you have erected. Fill your pots with compost, and plant the ferns so that there is enough room at the top for watering. (If you don't fancy getting dirty right now, just drop the plastic pots the ferns come in inside the pots you have chosen for your wall and re-pot them when you have the time and inclination.) Then hang the pots up on the nails or hooks.

   The single most important thing is to make sure the plants have a constant supply of water. You can do this by taking the whole lot down and giving them a good soak every few days or showering them in situ.

   If that's all a bit too much, you can get an equally Jurassic effect by grouping different pots of ferns together on the ground, or using hanging baskets.

A FEW OF MY
FAVOURITE FERNS
Ferns for the garden come in a plethora of forms, hardinesses, and weird and wonderful varieties. The varieties below are my 'fail-safes', because they are evergreen, suitable for dry or damp shade, and native to Britain, which I love.

The common polypody (*Polypodium vulgare*) Has beautiful, long lance-like fronds (fern leaves) that look like a thickly toothed comb. Height 10–50cm.
Soft shield fern (*Polystichum setiferum*) Has graceful arching fronds with a lovely soft texture. Height 60cm.
Hart's tongue fern (*Asplenium scolopendrium*) Has uncut strap-like fronds and looks fabulously primitive as a result. Height 45–60cm.

If you are putting ferns indoors, you can approach the idea with reckless abandon. I have found that any fern I randomly pick up on impulse from the nursery does well in a pot or hanging basket indoors. Just read the label and find out what it needs and how big it grows, and then act accordingly.

Succulent landscapes

When I was a child I used to spend hours poring over my grandmother's dressing table. It had tiny little boxes full of buttons, and china trays with jewellery, and little glasses with hairpins, and tiny silver photograph frames, and one of those old sets of hairbrush, comb and hand mirror that no one uses any more. Everything had a place, and each thing was precious – the dressing table was a landscape of objects. I do the same with tiny pots, grouping them together on a surface with anything pretty or meaningful that might otherwise spend its life forgotten at the back of a drawer.

Succulents lend themselves to these tabular landscapes, being small, fascinating and often geometrically formed. When they are viewed from above, the effect is not unlike that of a kaleidoscope or a Turkish tile.

THE LOWDOWN Succulents (which include cacti) are plants with fleshy leaves or stems, which can store water – and they need to, because they come from the desert. They come in a dazzling array of different forms, each adapted to this harsh environment. As far as 'care' is concerned, the only way you're likely to kill one of these plants is by giving it too much water. This makes them the best presents for plant murderers.

TIMING Any time.

YOU WILL NEED **A collection of succulents** They come in little pots all year round from most good nurseries, garden centres and some big DIY shops, and there are millions of them to choose from. Because you will treat them all in the same way, and they are not expensive, you can approach buying your collection in the same way as you might if you were presented with a blank cheque outside Tiffany's.
A wide, shallow pot One big enough for all your succulents, with drainage holes at the bottom.
Cactus compost Available in bags.
Pea gravel or grit

METHOD Fill the pot with cactus compost right up to the rim and plant the succulents carefully, making sure you don't overcrowd them: imagine a sparse, rocky / sandy landscape and position them accordingly. Then fill in all around them with the tiny gravel or grit. This is really important, as it stops them from rotting when you water them. If you're doing this in winter, don't water. In summer or spring, water them in lightly. (The same method applies when you're re-potting a single plant.)

I water my succulents once a fortnight in spring and summer by putting the whole pot in a tray of water for an hour or so. Stop watering in autumn and let them go to sleep.

Obviously, these plants grow, often bearing weird flowers and forming long stalks, as if they were trying to become trees.

MY FAVOURITE
SUCCULENTS

Echeveria These come in exquisite rosettes of waxy leaves, often with a glaucous bloom or red-tipped leaves.

Haworthia These have finely pointed thick warty leaves and look like strange sea creatures.

Pachyphytum oviferum The aptly named sugar-almond plant.

Sempervivum (houseleeks) These are in a class of their own because you can grow them inside or out.

AND MORE

I often leave these plants in their tiny plastic containers so that I can move them around in a never-ending game of chess. I also plant them up in shallow containers for presents. Troughs or dishes of succulents are ideal wedding presents – not least because they thrive on neglect (and newly married couples are always busy people).

How to cheat with garage flowers

This is hardly a recipe — more of a secret, really. It's my regular fallback for when I'm stuck for a present, and it works every time. I keep a pair of scissors and some string in my car and use this method for everyone — old or young, boys or girls.

A posy always looks charming and is immediately ready to be plonked into a little glass or milk jug as soon as it's received, unlike a larger bunch that has your host seeking out vases when they could be getting you a drink. This means that the flowers can be put out immediately, instead of the usual thing of being dumped in the sink, where they often languish for the entire evening. And men: although this can never replace carefully sourced, scented bouquets, it comes a pretty close second, and can be used as a more everyday thing to sweet-nothing your loved one.

TIMING   All the time.

YOU WILL NEED   **A bunch of supermarket or garage forecourt flowers**   It's best to go for a bunch of one type, but a mixture will do. One colour is better, but again a mixture will do. Flowers in bud are better, but open will do. You can (and should) use carnations and chrysanthemums as much as you want — and I rarely pay more than £1.99.
A pair of secateurs   Or use tough kitchen scissors.
A ball of ordinary unbleached garden twine   Or use post-office string, raffia in a natural colour or nice ribbon.
Five minutes

METHOD   Rip off the cellophane and chuck it. Remove any flowers you don't like or that have gone over. Strip the leaves off each stem and cut a length of string or ribbon. Gather the flowers into a tight bunch, grasping them as near to the base of each flower as you can, and tie them up nice and tightly as close to the top as possible, winding the string or ribbon around the stems three or four times and using a knot or a bow — whatever takes your fancy. When it's secure, cut the stems really quite short, making sure they're all the same length, so that you're left with a modish little posy that looks as if it comes from an expensive florist. That's it.

A cocktail for cut flowers

You can get pretty geeky about this, fiddling about with distilled water and correcting pH levels, but better to leave all that to florists, who have to make a living out of keeping flowers alive. In the spirit of moderation I'm setting down some basic things you can do to prolong vase life that don't involve thermometers, special equipment or clearing out your fridge.

THE LOWDOWN   Here are some basic rules:

1. If you're cutting your own flowers, do so in late morning, as this is when plant glucose levels are at their highest.
2. Make sure your scissors or secateurs are really sharp, and cut stems longer than you need.
3. Have a pail of water ready to put stems into immediately.
4. Strip off all foliage below the waterline.
5. Re-cut stems under water and put them straight into a vase.
6. In the vase, use water that is lukewarm and mix it with cut-flower cocktail (see below).
7. Change the water regularly, as soon as it shows signs of clouding.
8. Remove flowers as they go over, changing your vase and shortening stems to create a new arrangement if necessary.
9. Keep your vase in a cool place for most of the time – cut flowers will last much longer if they're in an unheated room.

TIMING   Any time.

YOU WILL NEED   **Water**
7Up Regular, not diet.
Liquid bleach Normal thin household bleach will do the trick.

METHOD   For every cup of water add 1 cup of 7Up and half a teaspoon of bleach. The 7Up will provide sugar and the bleach will keep the water clean.

A flower tower

This is a cheap, space-saving way to show off lots of plants — what you might call a 'centrepiece'. I often use this to hold a mixture of plants and food — the odd cupcake is a lovely surprise when you're not expecting to find one. I once found a mini-Bounty bar that I'd forgotten about hidden amongst something leafy on my flower tower, and it tasted more delicious for that reason alone. I think I'll hide money there next time.

TIMING   Any time.

YOU WILL NEED   **Plants** Ferns are great for a cascade effect, or a mixture of houseplants, trailing or otherwise.
7 small pots All the same size (terracotta ones can be bought very cheaply at garden centres).
4 trays The same shape (important) and same colour (less important), but different sizes, so that they all fit inside one another.
Blu-tack or double-sided tape

METHOD   Place three pots, upside down, on the largest tray, put a blob of Blu-tack or a strip of tape on each one and stick the next tray on top. Continue adding pots and trays until you have a tray pyramid (you may have to move the pots around to make it secure). Place plants around the edge of each tray to create a display.

Ivy praise

It's very easy to pass over something like ivy in favour of plants whose charms are more obviously alluring; but ivy, along with a few other evergreens, is the Bill Gates of the virgin's garden: the guy sitting at the front of the class with the thick glasses, the nerd who made good, the one you're kicking yourself about, wondering why the hell you didn't notice him before. For though ivy may never jump up and say 'Look at me', that is because it is doggedly, reliably doing its thing: clothing, cushioning, covering, protecting, providing a foil for the show-offs of the plant world or a background for your frolics. It works hard, it takes care of itself, it needs no coddling and it makes you look good; it's the perfect partner – the one that got away. It deserves eulogising, so here ivy becomes the main event.

THE LOWDOWN
Common English ivy (*Hedera helix*) is a vigorous self-clinging climber or trailing perennial, which comes from light woodland and scrambles over trees and rocks across Europe. It climbs by sending out special roots (called adventitious roots) from its stems that cling to a multitude of surfaces (have a close look next time you pass by some ivy). This climbing vine is actually the juvenile form of the plant, and it often sends out shoots that are mutations of itself. That shoot, removed, propagated and named, is a cultivar – and you see lots of these in the shops.

Ivy is deeply important for lots of birds and insects, who love it, and just wonderful for virgins because it is virtually indestructible, being utterly unfazed by dryness or lack of light. I grow my ivy inside and out, and neglect it appallingly, but the dead crispy bits only add to its charm.

TIMING
Spring or autumn.

YOU WILL NEED
Little pots of ivy Available from most garden centres (or get involved and choose some unusual ones from the specialist on page 262).
Container Stone, terracotta or whatever you like.
Compost A 50/50 mix of John Innes No. 2 and multi-purpose compost.
A handful of Osmacote granules (See page 229.)

METHOD
Ivy never tries to compete with anything visually, and when you're using it to decorate with, it is at its most lovely on its own. There is something fabulously unkempt and artless about a potful of trailing ivy: it looks ancient and rather scraggy, and so it should. Choose any large pot – stone is good, but terracotta is lovely too; a shallow urn is good, but not essential. Fill your container with the mixture of multi-purpose and John Innes No. 2, and the Osmacote granules (this plant is going to be here for some time) and plant your little ivies. I use nine or ten small pots of *Hedera helix* 'Glacier' to fill a large urn 45cm wide.

SOME FAVOURITE IVIES Small, for pots:

Hedera helix **'Glacier'** Really popular as a ground-cover plant because of its pale prettiness and non-invasive properties. Very Miss Havisham-ey.

H. helix **'Ivalace'** Lustrous dark green leaves with a crinkly disposition. It only grows to 1m, as it wastes so much energy looking pretty and lacy and interesting.

H. helix **'Buttercup'** Pale green to bright yellow (depending on how much sun it gets) with gorgeous large five-lobed leaves.

Big, for covering walls and anything ugly outside:

H. helix **'Oro di Bogliasco'** Sometimes sold as 'Goldheart', this thing shamelessly sports amazing yellow splotches in the middle of each leaf (though less so in deep shade).

H. hibernica **(Irish ivy)** An ivy that really will cover everything in sight if you give it half a chance. It's dark green, mysterious and beautiful.

Easy party flowers

I should qualify this title by saying that this is the easiest way of giving a room that 'done' look that evokes thoughts of 'I wonder who did the flowers?'.

Party flowers are a doddle if you've got lots of cash: just buy armfuls of lovely bouquets and put them in matching, gorgeous vases — job done. The method below is my answer to the problem of not owning all those receptacles and being either too skint or too mean to afford the masses of blooms required to fill them. Instead of vases I use fruit, and the kookiness of the display allows me to get away with a sparseness that will save me the kind of money that makes this more than worth the effort. Repeat the arrangement to create an impression of opulence. Keep colours bold and bright; it doesn't matter if things clash; the only prerequisite is that the stems must be tough enough to stand up straight with very little support.

TIMING   Any time.

FOR EACH DISPLAY
YOU WILL NEED

Flowers
1 stem of something weird and wonderful, e.g. *Strelitzia reginae* (bird-of-paradise flower), 'Star Gazer' lily or *Zantedeschia* (arum lily).
1 stem of something tall and long and poker-like, e.g. *Eremurus* (foxtail lily), *Gladiolus* (only the giant ones will do), *Hedychium* (ginger lily), *Kniphofia* (red-hot poker) or large lupin.
1 circular or ball-like inflorescence, e.g. *Allium*, *Agapanthus* or any *Protea*.
1 palm leaf, e.g. *Washingtonia* or *Howea forsteriana* (Kentia palm).
1 big fat leaf, e.g. *Alocasia*, *Calathea*, *Colocasia*, *Fatsia* or *Hosta*.
1 large watermelon or pineapple
1 shallow dish A bowl, plate or pot holder; this must be large enough to hold the fruit you choose. I use plastic faux-terracotta saucers.
An apple corer
Optional extras Sparklers, wooden skewers and some smaller soft fruit.

METHOD   Slice the bottom off the watermelon or pineapple and place it in the shallow dish, so that it is stable and any juice is contained. This is your 'vase'.

Decide roughly what you want your arrangement to look like and bore a hole for each stem in the fruit with an apple corer, remembering to think about what angle you want the stem to come out at.

I go really tall sometimes with the ginger lily, so the whole thing ends up around 2m high; then I put in the strelitzia, at half the height, and then the allium pom-pom — all at different levels and coming out at different angles — with a palm leaf sticking out at about strelitzia height and the remaining leaf really low down on the fruit to hide any messy bits at the bottom. Then I put in three sticks, again at different levels, each with a plum or clementine stuck on the end of it, and then maybe a sparkler or two — or even an incense stick.

The day after the party, dismantle the display, put the stems in water and eat the fruit — unless others have already had the same idea the night before.

Mausoleum fun

On long summer holidays in North Wales I always collected rows and rows of dead insects on window frames to be pored over on rainy days. It's a bit of a habit, and I include it here for two reasons: firstly because on your gardening forays you will inevitably start picking up tiny things like winged seeds and dried calyces that will need a home – if only for a while – and secondly because there is something really priceless about watching your city friends peering intently through a magnifying glass at the thorax of a bumble bee.

TIMING Any time.

YOU WILL NEED **Some old print shelves** These are what newspapers used to keep their letter blocks in before these were made redundant by computers. You can find them in markets and antique shops, or it's worth ringing up your local rag to see if they have any lying around.
Some white or pale-coloured paint
Beady eyes

METHOD Paint your shelves – this is boring but important, because they are usually stained dark with ink and you want to be able to see your treasures. Fix them to a wall or make a table top out of them by laying a piece of glass over the top. When you are messing around with your plants, keep an eye out for interesting things and fill the compartments with anything you find. Seeds are brilliant for this, as are leaves and flowers that fascinate you. I also use these shelves for anything tiny that I have lying around and can't bear to throw away. Keep a magnifying glass handy, and if you collect dead insects, I suggest using a Collins Gem for identification purposes.

CAMPANULA
CARPATICA

An easy dinner table

When you're entertaining guests and you want things looking chic, there's a balance to be struck between things looking too 'done' and not making any effort at all. While it's deceptively simple to put flowers on a table so that it ends up looking like something straight out of a magazine photo-shoot (just keep blooms low and tightly packed), it's also easy to give the impression that you spent oodles of time and money doing it.
I don't like this — it feels uncomfortable, no matter how informal the arrangement is — so here I offer some ideas for table arrangements that look smart and sophisticated and take no time at all, with the added benefit that you won't be seen as a try-hard. The other good thing is that because you're not working with cut flowers there's no preparation involved, and the decoration will keep for much longer.

TIMING   Any time.

YOU WILL NEED   **Little pots of whatever plant you choose** This will depend on the time of year. Those small pots of spiky grass that are sold next to the till at massive DIY stores are a real winner, or anything pretty that takes your fancy in the garden centre.
The same number of plant pots or containers for your bought plants to go inside You can buy small bog-standard terracotta pots for next to nothing and they're always useful; or get those small galvanised metal buckets that you can buy at supermarkets in sets of three, complete with tray; or even better, if you have a collection of china or pottery bowls deep enough for the little plastic pots use these — the point is that it's good if they are all the same, or similar.
A bag of sphagnum moss (Optional.)

METHOD   It hardly needs saying, but put one potted plant inside each decorative container, laying torn-off pieces of moss on top if any ugly bits need hiding, and arrange them on your table. If your guests compliment you, pull a plant out and show them there's no excuse for an unlovely table.

How to make cheap vases

Even if you hate doing crafty stuff like this, the money-saving aspect will convert you.
You can never have enough vases and they're expensive to buy, so enamel all the old
bottles and jars you have lying around and spend your precious money on plants and
flowers to fill them. Enamel paint creates a lovely opaque look that still allows light to
shine through, and if you use coloured glass, so much the better.

TIMING
Any time.

YOU WILL NEED
Old bottles and jars Labels removed, thoroughly clean and dry; the more
coloured ones you have the better.
A tin of Dulux Trade Super Grip Primer
White enamel paint
A damp cloth
An old plate One you don't mind getting paint on.

METHOD
With each bottle or jar, pour a little of the primer into it and swish it around.
This will prime the glass for the enamel paint. Pour out any excess and turn
the bottle or jar upside down for a few hours. When it is dry, do the same
thing with a generous amount of enamel paint so that the inside of the
receptacle is fully coated. Tidy up any drips from the rim with a damp cloth
and leave the bottle or jar to dry overnight on the plate.

Aloe in a bowl

I got this idea from a shop window display and it's the easiest way to sex up a room. The idea of a 'desert in a bowl' is nothing new (I remember my granny had one when I was very little), but having more than two of anything identical instantly elevates it from a mere curiosity to a design statement.

THE LOWDOWN
Aloe vera is native to dry areas in South Africa, so as long as it doesn't get frosted or damp, it will survive perfectly happily in this country. We are by now all aware of its healing properties, soothing sunburn and sealing wounds, but for me it comes into its own as a houseplant – particularly if displayed as described below.

TIMING
Any time.

YOU WILL NEED
3 small aloe plants Available indoors at most good garden centres. You don't have to use aloe – any succulent will look great.
A bag of pale, fine sand Sold in garden centres for children's sandpits.
3 identical glass containers Fishbowls are good, or tall, straight vases.

METHOD
Put a layer of sand into each glass container and bury the plant in its pot, so that the plastic is completely hidden and the sand covers the top of the compost.

    Place your bowls in a line, wherever they look the most striking. That's it. All you need to remember is to water the plants just a little (too much water will cause them to rot) once a week between spring and autumn. Give them hardly any water all winter, when they are resting; if your room is baking hot from the central heating, keep them in an unheated room during this period.

    You should also give your aloes a liquid feed of something like Baby Bio, just the once, when spring has sprung.

AND MORE
In summer your plants will probably make babies – little offshoots at the base. You can gently tease these away from the parent, leave them for a day to dry and then put them into a little pot filled with two-thirds multi-purpose compost and one-third grit or sand. Water them and leave them in the warm to take root. Remember to soothe the bereft parent by giving it some liquid feed when you return it to its pot.

Seedhead theatre

Certain plants are at their most beautiful in death, and some are obliging enough to withstand the ravages of winter and stay upright and gorgeous, especially in the early morning when covered with frost. These plants are also wonderful when cut and brought indoors, left natural or sprayed in gold or silver, providing everlasting decorations that are perfect for Christmas or New Year time – and if you train a light up from underneath them the shadows created make fabulous pictures.

THE LOWDOWN
Dried seedheads are big business and you can buy them at florists and markets, or grow your own. Or if you're given a bunch of flowers, when they're over just hang them up in a dry place and see what happens.

TIMING
Seedheads last for ever.

METHOD
Dead flowers obviously don't need water, so place them wherever you want; or if you're growing them, just leave them in the garden. I use bulldog clips to attach mine to a big standard lamp, which causes dramatic shadows on a bare wall.

MY FAVOURITE SEEDHEADS
Achillea Lovely flat flowerheads in colours ranging from creamy white to deep maroon. All achilleas provide structural seedheads after they're over. They need good drainage, especially in winter.

Allium The stars of the show where seedheads are concerned. The best ones are *A. cristophii* and *A. schubertii*, which look like exploding stars (see opposite). If you buy or grow one plant for this purpose, make it one of these.

Echinacea These daisies are the ultimate prairie plants for late-summer and early-autumn splendour. They have pink and purple or orange flowers that become utterly exquisite in death.

Eryngium (sea holly) These have gorgeous prickly foliage and steel or violet flowers that form a thistly head. They are all spectacular, but *E. giganteum* 'Silver Ghost' is a particular favourite.

Grasses The flowers of many ornamental grasses dry brilliantly and quiver as you walk by, even when dead.

Lunaria annua (honesty) Really easy to grow, this has exquisite papery, flat seed cases, which are opaque and look like the moon.

Rudbeckia These are lovely daisies that bloom from late summer and into autumn, with flower colours ranging from pale yellow to burnt umber and every shade in between, and amazing, dark, sometimes conical seedheads. *R. fulgida* var. *deamii* is my favourite, with a beauteous black seedhead.

Sanguisorba (burnet) They look a little like giant matchsticks, and have unshowy flowers clustered on the end of long elegant stems.

Sedum Gorgeous fleshy foliage in beautiful colours before you even see the flowers, which persist throughout the winter long after they've faded. I love *S.* 'Bertram Anderson' and *S. spectabile* 'Iceberg'.

Hanging jam jars

I'm always looking for ways to get things off surfaces and up at eye level. Unused cut herbs, flowers I've picked and want to admire while I do the washing up — I hang these on window latches and any hook I can find. And because I am a cheapskate I use old jars, which are perfect for this purpose, as they have a rim. (I am also addicted to raspberry jam, which helps.)

TIMING   Any time.

YOU WILL NEED   **Clean, empty jars**
String

METHOD   For each jar, take a length of string, double it up and put it around the neck of the jar under the rim, leaving enough string to suspend the jar with. Thread the ends through the loop and pull tight. Tie a knot to create a loop from the two loose ends, and hang the jar to anything resembling a hook. The wall will keep it upright enough for you to fill it with water and add your flower pickings.

If you don't want people to know you've been eating Dulce de Leche on the sly, or have reservations about the aesthetic potential of displaying your daisies in a jar of Grey Poupon, see the recipe for cheap vases on page 52.

Budget bedding

Bedding allows you to behave like a fashion designer and have a go at devising a 'look' for the season. Think 'mood', think 'texture', think (dare I say it?) 'colourways' ...

Bedding plants are the best way by far of souping up your living space on a crazy whim for next to nothing. They allow you to play with the latest colours and shapes in the same way you do by rushing to Topshop for the latest trend on the cheap, knowing that you may tire of it and throw it out.

THE LOWDOWN I'm talking about those polystyrene cells that are sold in vast quantities in garden centres, filled with small plants and labelled 'bedding'. The plants raised inside these cells are known as plugs, as they are used by gardeners to fill gaps in their borders (flowerbeds to you and me) and by window-box and container-garden aficionados to create temporary displays. They are cheap because they are young and therefore small, taking up less compost than more mature specimens, and they've been grown in a factory-like environment to hit the shelves en masse and be planted immediately.

Traditionally, the word 'bedding' encompasses annuals or half-hardy plants that add summer colour, but you can get frost-hardy perennial plants sold as bedding which, if you look after them properly, can be wonderful permanent additions. Either way, bedding plants are for me a cheap, easy way of discovering new plants and deciding whether I'm enamoured with them enough to grow them again, give them a permanent place in my life or order a more expensive, less ubiquitous variety of the same thing. If I end up deciding against them, I've lost nothing except £2.99 and the time it took to put the thing in a pot.

TIMING Spring and summer, though there are plenty of cheap plugs on sale throughout autumn and winter, which I use as temporary plants.

YOU WILL NEED **Bedding plants** The cheapest will be the plug plants described above. This is a great way to experiment with something you've never tried before. Buy as many plants as you have room for – and then some more. I tend to go all out on one species all in the same colour, but just choose whatever tickles your artistic tastebuds.
Containers such as window boxes Or gaps in your flowerbed.
Multi-purpose compost If you are using containers.

METHOD Planting distances are always printed on the label and should be adhered to as far as possible as the plant will then have room to spread and the display will last longer. Fill your containers (if you are using them) with compost and push each plant out of its cell from the underside and fill up your pots or flowerbed so that the plants are snug but not crammed, making sure that the compost or soil is nice and firm around each plug. Water them in thoroughly, and then keep them watered and happy in an area suitable for whichever plant you have chosen. For continual flowers, be sure to deadhead (see page 231).

MY FAVOURITE
BEDDING PLANTS

Aster
Begonia
Bellis perennis (daisy)
Calendula (marigold)
Dianthus barbatus (sweet william)
Erysimum cheiri (wallflower)
Fuchsia
Gazania
Impatiens (busy Lizzie)
Lobelia
Nemesia
Osteospermum
Pelargonium (popularly known as geranium)
Petunia
Primula (primrose)
Ranunculus asiaticus (Persian buttercup)
Viola × *wittrockiana* (pansy)
Zinnia

Cyclamen addiction

Before Christmas I go to the market and buy at least four trays of cyclamen in fabulously anarchic clashing colours (all at the red end of the spectrum), with the idea of potting them up in small containers and giving them to friends and family. I do this every year, really believing that I have Christmas sorted, but somewhere between getting the things home and putting them in containers a switch trips in my brain and I become too attached to them to give them to anyone. To this day, I have only ever been able to give away one plant, under extreme emotional pressure. I don't know why these little, butterfly-like blooms with their beautifully patterned, heart-shaped leaves should so hold me to ransom; they just do.

THE LOWDOWN

Cyclamen are perennials and they come from a wide range of different habitats in Europe, Asia and Africa, but the ones we see most often originate from the Mediterranean woodland, so they like dappled light, shelter from strong winds and, most importantly, well-drained soil.

The other thing about cyclamen is that they are tuberous, and don't like being disturbed, so although it's perfectly possible to plant a garden-centre cyclamen outside once you've finished with it indoors, I don't usually bother, and if I'm looking for cyclamen that I want to spend my life with (some tubers have been dated at over 100 years old) I tend to spend a bit more time and money at a specialist nursery. So buy cheap ones with abandon and do some or all of the following.

TIMING

Autumn to winter.

WAYS WITH
CYCLAMEN

Here are a few ways in which I display my garden-centre-bought trays of mini-blooms.

* Pot up in recycled tin cans (my favourites are pilchards and Heinz cream of tomato soup) by consuming the contents (tricky with pilchards), drilling a hole in the bottom of the can, filling with multi-purpose compost with added grit and putting a plant in each one.

* Do the spring-bulbs-in-a-basket thing (see page 157) and either plant your cyclamen in a plastic-lined basket or don't bother to take them out of their plastic pots and just put the whole lot in a basket deep and wide enough to take a few little plants – the leaves will do the work of hiding the ugly plastic pot rims. This method has the added bonus that you can remove the pots to water them, so they don't get waterlogged and you don't have to get your hands dirty.

* Do the classic Victorian thing and use a straight-sided china bowl. People keep cyclamen alive for years in these receptacles. I would be tortured by the thought of over-watering, though, because of the lack of drainage holes. So

either make sure your china bowl is a 'planter' (with holes) or just put the plastic pots directly inside it for your temporary display. I have done this same thing with bowls of every description – using stones to prop up the pots inside and moss to hide anything unsightly – including coffee mugs and large vintage tea cups (white cyclamen look gorgeous in these).

※ And if you can bear to give away a plant or two, use any of the above methods, or just tie a jolly ribbon round a mini-pot of lipstick-red cyclamen, and give one to every person who invites you round to their house for a mince pie before Christmas.

Cyclamen can be kept inside or outside – just remember to deadhead them (see page 231) and they'll keep on flowering until you're sick of the sight of them.

MY FAVOURITE
CYCLAMEN
My favourite cyclamen for all year round, which I have in pots and love and care for and ogle over like the misers you read about in storybooks, are as follows (naturally, all of them have scent):

Cyclamen cilicium f. album Has pure white honey-scented flowers in September and October and is considered hardy by most growers.
C. cyprium Obviously from Cyprus, and again frost-tender. Has really strongly scented white flowers in October and November.
C. persicum f. albidum Spring flowering with a pure white flower and strong lily-of-the-valley scent. Frost-tender, so best grown with some shelter.
C. pseudibericum 'Roseum' Flowers in February (yay!) and is hardy in mild areas. Has rose-pink flowers with a strong scent.
C. repandum Flowers in April and May and has carmine-coloured, violet-scented flowers.

Hops for decoration and sedation

I love this plant. It's like playdough: you can make it into something different every time. Everyone should grow a hop: you can have it in a pot or in the ground and have your wicked way with it all summer long. A hop is one of the few plants that look really fabulous dried, and it provides you with a ready-made garland for Christmas. Both leaves and flowers are green and unbelievably pretty, and a pillow stuffed with hop flowers sends you into dreamy sleep.

THE LOWDOWN

Humulus lupulus (hop) is a twining hardy perennial that grows wild in wood-landish places in most northern temperate regions. It will grow up anything (including string) for up to 6m, and because it is perennial it will disappear in winter and come back again the following year, so you can literally play sculptor and make something different with it every year. You can buy *Humulus lupulus* in most good garden centres or order it online. Make sure you get a female, because only the females have the beautiful flowers. If you buy the yellow cultivar (called 'Aureus'), you'll get the best leaf colour in full sun. *Humulus lupulus* likes good soil and full sun or partial shade. Plant it in spring and keep it watered, and by summer it will have romped to the heavens.

TIMING

Spring.

YOU WILL NEED

As many *Humulus lupulus* plants as will fit in your space
Containers I have two plants in a deep pot measuring 35cm in diameter.
Compost Use John Innes No. 2 with one-third multi-purpose compost.
Osmacote granules (See page 229.) Use a couple of handfuls.
Something for the plant to climb up I use string.

METHOD

If you're using a container, mix the compost with the Osmacote, remove the plant from its plastic pot and plant your hop in it. Make sure there's enough space between the top of the compost and the rim of the pot, so that it can hold some water, giving the water time to sink into the compost rather than run down the sides of the container.

   If you're planting in the ground, put a handful of Osmacote granules in the hole before you plant.

   Next, you will need to tie the plant gently to whatever you want it to climb up. By all means begin your hoppy adventure with a large pot and a simple wigwam (see A runner bean wigwam, page 118), but you could think much bigger – all you need is a trellis, pergola or framework of some kind. You could even create a temporary hop shade, simply by suspending a network of strings from a single hook high up on a wall. The possibilities, as you may imagine, are endless. Make sure you keep the plant watered.

Here are a few ideas:

❃ To make a hop pillow, take handfuls of hop flowers (from a female plant) and allow them to dry out for a few days. Cut out two squares of soft fabric – muslin is nice. Sew the two squares together around the edge of three sides, turn out and press; then stuff with hop flowers and sew the last side shut. Put head on pillow and shut eyes … voilà.

❃ To make a hop garland, cut down your whole hop plant at the base at the end of summer, or when you deem it to have enough flowers, and carefully tease each stem away from its support. Some of it will inevitably be damaged, but it *so* doesn't matter. Take the bines into your house and drape them over anything – your kitchen dresser, hooks in the ceiling, a mantelpiece, your four-poster bed … They will slowly dry naturally, dying a beautiful death. Make sure they're out of the way, as they'll be damaged if people bash into them. At Christmas they will still look beautiful, but you could spray some gold at this point if you want things a little more festive.

❃ If you only have room for one hop plant but are really nutty about having hop bines everywhere then fear not, because you can order them from a hop farm (ask Mr Google).

How to age terracotta pots

This is an age-old trick for making new pots look not so new. The flaky look is infinitely preferable to me than the startling orange of brand-new terracotta.

THE LOWDOWN — Yoghurt attracts algae, lichen and moss to clean pots. I don't know the exact science but I presume that it provides nutrients for the spores.

TIMING — I always do this in spring.

YOU WILL NEED — **Terracotta pots**
Paintbrush
Live full-fat yoghurt or buttermilk

METHOD — Simply paint the outside of the pots with a good coating of the yoghurt or buttermilk and leave them outside. To speed up the process, make sure that the pot stays on the damp side; that means leaving it in the shade and spraying it with water from time to time until nature has built up the patina you want.

I don't always do this, often planting up my pots immediately and leaving them in the sun if the plant inside wants that. This sometimes makes the yoghurt dry and flaky initially, but I find that as long as the pot is watered regularly it still ages nicely, especially when the plant grows and provides shade for it.

AND MORE — There are various other ways of doing this, like diluting the yoghurt with water, mixing it with bits of moss or dirt, or using organic fertiliser instead.

Daisies for paving

I absolutely hate myself for having my back yard paving pointed; there's not a crack to be seen. If you have paving stones with cracks between them, or a wall with missing mortar, then lucky, lucky you, because you can grow a plant that will spread to other cracks, softening everything in its wake. I have to be content with having my daisies in a container until enough years have passed for cracks to appear.

THE LOWDOWN
This plant is a perennial daisy, from a genus commonly known as fleabane. It has no common name specific to it, so you'll need to ask for *Erigeron karvinskianus* – a bit of a mouthful, but worth it. This thing grows like a weed – the nurseries must make a mint on it – so if you can find it in someone else's garden, ask if you can dig a bit up and plant that. It comes from Mexico but is fully hardy in the UK, and bears loads of little flopping daisies all summer, which start off white and then go pink as if they've been kissed by a fairy wearing lipstick.

TIMING
Spring.

YOU WILL NEED
1 *Erigeron karvinskianus* plant These are available in early summer from garden centres.
A crack in your paving or wall

METHOD
It's best to start this plant off in the shade, where it can get some moisture. It will then make its way to other places in your outside space by dispersing its seed. So don't try to put it everywhere, because some places you choose are bound to be unsuitable and you will waste money. Make sure there is some soil between the paving stones or bricks, and squish the plant in, dividing it if necessary (see page 160).

Be nice to it initially, keeping it watered until it's well established. Eventually, if you've chosen a place that's moist enough, you will be able to leave it alone and let nature provide for it. Even if you've chosen the wrong place initially, if you keep it watered in the first year it will self-seed.

AND MORE
As an alternative, you can buy the seed of this plant, mix it with soil and rub it into the cracks in your wall or paving.

The best wedding presents

Wedding lists are all very well, but I mainly go off-list — it's much nicer for the bride and groom, and far more economical for me. A wedding present should be something that lasts a long time, is utterly inoffensive and reminds the recipients of you. An alpine trough meets all these criteria, and always delights.

THE LOWDOWN
Alpine plants are like jewels — tough and beautiful. They are low-growing little things which have adapted to survive the harshest of conditions by clinging to rocks. Many of our common garden plants have alpine cousins that look like them, only in miniature.

Alpines are very hardy; they will withstand any amount of cold and wind, but they cannot abide wetness (snow, ice and stony soil keep things very dry on mountains), which makes an alpine trough a perfect candidate for a balcony or windowsill.

You can order ready-planted alpine troughs from specialist nurseries made from a material called tufa, which looks just like rock but weighs a squillionth of the real thing. These troughs come in all shapes and sizes, from very small to very large.

The ready-made troughs can cost anything from £50 upwards, but you can plant up your own for a fraction of this, and nobody need know.

TIMING
Spring to summer.

YOU WILL NEED
Alpine plants You can buy a selection of alpines in six-packs from good garden centres for under £10. They're all different, and choosing is the hardest part of this project.

A container You can get tufa containers from specialist nurseries or find something different. The container should be wide and shallow. I often use ordinary terracotta shallow pots. Whatever you choose, make sure that it has a hole or holes in the bottom and won't crack in a severe winter (so if you're using terracotta, make sure it says 'frost-resistant' on the label).

Crocks (old bits of broken pot) or some gravel To line the bottom of your container.

Really gritty compost I use a half-and-half mixture of multi-purpose and horticultural grit.

A handful of slow-release fertiliser granules such as Osmacote (See page 229.)

Some interesting stones Broken bits of slate are ideal, pebbles and bits of rock are good — you're making a mini mountainside.

Some small gravel (pea-sized) or horticultural grit To sprinkle over the top.

METHOD   Fill the container with a layer of crocks or gravel. This will provide really superb drainage. Then put a layer of mixed compost and fertiliser granules on top and either a) arrange your plants artfully, filling in gaps and firming them in well, and then arrange your stones between them; or b) stick pieces of slate in the compost on their sides, all going one way to re-create the look of mountain scree, fill the crevices with compost, packing it into the cracks, and then plant your alpines inside these cracks (you can be quite rough with them, squishing them in and pushing them down firmly). In both cases, cover every bit of bare compost with gravel or grit so that it comes right up around the base of the plants – this will stop water from lingering near the foliage, which they hate. Give the whole thing a good water, watering gently around the plants rather than on top of them.

    Get the present round to its recipient before the wedding, along with a little bottle of general-purpose liquid fertiliser to be applied each spring after the first year and instructions that they are to water their alpine trough regularly (i.e. once a week or so), at least until the plants are established.

AND MORE   Alternatively you can give a small tree in a pot. Something like a citrus is good, although it needs bringing indoors in winter, or a little Japanese maple (*Acer palmatum*), which looks like a bonsai tree only larger, can live in a large pot permanently and is one of the most beautiful things on the planet. Mail-order companies will deliver these for you, complete with personalised message and a big bow, and you need think no more about it (see Suppliers, page 262).

Pumpkins, squashes and gourds

Dense, waxy, sweet roasted butternut squash is one of my favourite comfort foods, but I don't grow these pumpkins, squashes and gourds for their eating value. This is principally because the ones I want to grow are far too fabulous to be mutilated, and besides, their uneven surfaces make them a nightmare to peel.

Instead, I urge you to grow just one squash or pumpkin for its ornamental value. If you treat it right, the thing will shoot up – if it's a vining variety, it will start galloping over everything, triffid-like – and provide gorgeous foliage and extraordinary fruits to decorate with. This project is perfect for a piece of earth you don't quite know what to do with yet, or an area where you can place a large pot.

THE LOWDOWN
Squashes are all species of the genus *Cucurbita*, and are generally divided into two groups: summer squash (to which our familiar marrows and courgettes belong), which are harvested in summer, and winter squash (such as butternut squash and pumpkin), which are harvested at the end of summer and therefore have a much harder skin, and flesh that needs cooking. There are also very decorative squashes, generally deemed inedible, which are labelled gourds. You can buy seedlings of all these at nurseries and garden centres, but growing them from seed is really easy and deeply rewarding, because they grow so fast.

TIMING
Late spring to early summer.

YOU WILL NEED
Seeds Go out and have a lovely time at a garden centre choosing a packet of seeds with a pretty picture. There are usually packets of mixed winter squash seeds available, which will give you lots of different varieties. Pay attention to size and growth habit, which will be listed on the seed packet. If you have a small space, choose a vining variety, so that you can control where it goes. I often go for a mixture of inedible gourds.
Fertile soil These plants like the good life, so if you are planting out in the open, dig in some organic matter, such as well-rotted manure. If using a container, make it a really large one and use multi-purpose compost.
The right temperature These plants will get nuked if you sow them too early and they get cold, so wait until it's nice and warm outside. That means late spring or early summer, when the soil feels warm to the touch.
A sunny sheltered site I use my balcony.

METHOD
Sow three seeds about 2cm deep, all together, water them in and put an up-ended jam jar over the top to keep the seedlings warm and provide a humid atmosphere for germination. Each seed will put out two seed leaves to start the plant off, and then start growing its proper leaves. Select the plant you like best and remove the other two, and discard the jar at this point. Keep the soil or compost just moist.

If you've sown a galloping gourd, there are loads of ways to train these plants and keep them 'tidy', including pinning the shoots down with tent pegs in a circle and making tepee-like structures with bamboo sticks. Smaller cultivars will even grow up string if you help them a little by tying them in every so often. The point here is that there are no hard and fast rules; the joy of these plants is that if you let them go, they will trail and wind over everything, creating a wonderful, jungle-like effect.

To get wacky winter squash to decorate your home all winter, you need to leave the fruits on the plant as long as possible before there's any danger of frost, so that their skins harden naturally. Eventually you will see cracks appearing on the skin, and this is a good time to cut the fruits off the plant, with a long piece of stem attached. Cure them by leaving them in the sun for about ten days (or in the event of bad weather, bring them indoors and keep them on a sunny windowsill).

AND MORE   It's possible to dry the fruits out completely and wax them or paint with shellac to create lovely presents. I don't have the cool, dark cellar that would be necessary for this, but I love to pile them up in large wooden bowls and put them on the floor, Ali Baba style, for indoor picnics with candles and warming pumpkin soup when it's wet and cold outside.

How to make a Christmas wreath

This is not just for the realm of the ultra-organised. Wreaths are deliciously easy to make and welcome you into your own home after a long day at work, which is delightfully self-respecting and cheery.

TIMING   Winter.

YOU WILL NEED   **A good armful of evergreen foliage** This could, of course, be holly, but pine, cedar, fir, juniper, box, bay, eucalyptus, sage and even magnolia or camellia are all possibilities. Either get this from a flower market or your own garden, or beg from a kind neighbour.
Strong scissors or secateurs
A roll of thin wire Like copper wire but preferably black or green.
A wreath form Available from some florists, markets and art or DIY stores – or you could make your own, like I do, using thick wire, fastening the ends with thin wire.
Other optional embellishments See below.
Wire cutters

METHOD   First you have to make lots of little sprigs out of your greenery. Snap off small pieces of foliage 10–15cm long and wire them together into a thick little bundle. Make lots of these bundles and then begin adding them to your wreath by laying each bundle along the length of the wreath form and tightly wrapping it with wire from halfway up its length to the bottom. Don't cut the wire, but add another bundle, using the top of this second bundle to hide the bottom half of the previous one, and carry on winding the wire around this bundle until you reach the bottom of it, at which point add another, and so on until you have covered everything. This is your basic wreath and you can either adulterate it with whatever turns you on or leave it as it is.

MY FAVOURITE ADORNMENTS   Obviously berries are a must for some, and you can go down the classic route with holly or pyracantha berries, or use something else, such as rosehips. If you want to branch out a little, I suggest glass beads threaded on to wire, fruit such as dried citrus or pomegranates, kumquats, flowers poked into the foliage such as amaryllis, roses or anything blowsy that you can get from the garage, or nuts and acorns – either au naturel or sprayed gold or silver (bore holes in these with a very fine drill bit, and thread wire through before attaching them to the wreath) … You get the idea: once you have the basic wreath the sky's the limit.

Lastly, it's sometimes nice to spray the whole thing with white or silver florists' spray to give it a snowy feel.

AND MORE   You can create garlands and swags in exactly the same way, either by making a frame out of wire or – much simpler – by wiring your foliage to a length of rope that you've swagged around your fireplace or wherever. It's lovely to do this with aromatic foliage like bay, to get a nice heady fug going.

Eat

I'm not the kind of person with either the commitment or the inclination to become self-sufficient. Even though it's perfectly possible to keep an entire family in vegetables from a few pots on a balcony, there is for me a balance to be struck between the aesthetic and the practical (particularly in a small space). Being a greedy person, eating is one of my greatest pleasures, and I grow plenty of edible plants that both look beautiful and taste delicious.

Here are some recipes for easy, edible things to grow, from essential kitchen herbs to soft summer fruit. There is very little to beat coming home after a long day and flaking out with a bowl of home-grown raspberries, or gently nudging new parents off the subject of their children by getting them to pick their own salad leaves, or having someone fall head over heels in love with you after a few precious freshly cut asparagus spears.

Everyone knows that this kind of food tends to taste better, but what those who grow their own don't talk about so often is that it also *feels* better when the eating of a fruit, vegetable or herb becomes the consummation of a process that started only a few weeks before with the sprinkling of some seed.

Peppermint creams and minty things

I might have put this piece on mint in any section. Mint finds itself scattered on food, crushed in dressings, infused in oils and even sprinkled in the bath, but most often plunged into drinks, cold and hot. I wouldn't dream of telling you how to make mint tea, but it is worth knowing how to grow mint so that you can always have it around, and most importantly, so that you can make oil for mint creams, which are deeply delicious and for me reminiscent of childhood cooking sessions.

THE LOWDOWN Mint (*Mentha*) is a perennial plant that spreads using rhizomes (underground stems). Add to this the fact that it thrives on very poor soil, in sun or shade, and you have something that could potentially take over your space if it's not kept under control. (Gardeners call this kind of plant a thug.) For this reason it's best to grow mint in pots or, if you're planting it in the ground, to plant it in its pot, unless of course you want a garden full of mint (which would be a bit boring, but no bad thing).

There are lots of different varieties of mint, each with its own distinct flavour, and other plants, such as lemon balm (*Melissa officinalis*), which are not mint but are often used as such. The most readily available from shops are spearmint (*Mentha spicata*), peppermint (*Mentha × piperita*), apple mint (*Mentha suaveolens*) and bergamot (*Monarda didyma*). The point is that they all contain menthol and other things that make them 'minty', and it's worth buying lots of different plants to see which one you like best.

Pot them up in terracotta pots using multi-purpose compost or plant out in any old garden soil and keep them watered, because they're thirsty plants. In summer, they all produce clustered flowers, usually lilac in colour, which are lovely in salads or for putting in little vases.

I have pots of different mint indoors during the growing season, because they smell fabulous and I want them close to hand. I then put them outdoors for the winter and forget about them and they always come up again the following spring, even though they get no attention.

TIMING Spring and summer.

YOU WILL NEED **Fresh mint leaves** You don't have to use peppermint – any mint will do and I often use a mixture.
A clean jam jar
120ml organic sweet almond oil Available from health food shops, often in the beauty section.
A piece of muslin
200g icing sugar
White from 1 large egg, beaten

METHOD   Pack the jam jar full with chopped fresh mint leaves and heat the almond oil so that it's just warm. I put the oil in an oven-proof measuring jug in my oven, turn the dial to the lowest temperature possible, and then wait until the pilot light goes out (about 6 minutes). Pour the oil over the leaves in the jar and stir it with a clean spoon to get rid of any air bubbles. When it is cool, screw the lid on the jar and put it in the dark for about a month to allow the mint to infuse the oil, then strain the oil through muslin, squeezing out the last drop.

Sift the icing sugar into the beaten egg white until you have a stiff paste, and add the oil to taste. Roll out the paste as you would dough and cut it into shapes. Leave the creams on greaseproof paper covered with a tea towel overnight to harden.

AND MORE   You can produce essential oil in this way from any aromatic culinary herb. Rosemary, lavender and thyme are great subjects for this treatment, and little bottles of essential oil are much better gifts than the no-longer-special idea of herb-infused olive oil – so ubiquitous now it is considered more of an insult than a present.

83

Chives

Not just for your soured cream dip, chives are an excellent plant for the windowsill,
as they serve the dual purpose of providing a harvest of something to eat and something
to look at. Grow them in a pot that's somewhere easily accessible, or in a patch of earth
near your kitchen with fertile soil and a bit of shade.

THE LOWDOWN   Chives (*Allium schoenoprasum*) are a member of the onion family, as their taste suggests, but this does not preclude them from being used ornamentally, and I often see chives edging the borders in very grand gardens indeed. This is because their onioniness is not overpowering and their flowers (they come in purple, pink and white) are wonderfully pretty.

TIMING   Start in late spring.

YOU WILL NEED   **A packet of chive seed from the garden centre** Choose your colour.
A window box or pot
Multi-purpose compost

METHOD   Fill your window box or pot with compost and make some shallow drills – gardening speak for dipping your finger in up to the first joint and pulling it through the soil from one end of the pot to the other in a straight line. Now sprinkle the seeds in these little ditches thinly. Bring the displaced soil back over the top of them and pat gently. Water with the fine rose of a watering can, so as not to displace any of the seeds, leave them on your windowsill and wait.

Chives like a partially shaded spot if possible and loads of water (those leaves are lush). When they're growing, feed them once a week or so with a liquid fertiliser to keep them really gorgeous. They grow up to 30cm high and you can cut the whole lot down to within 3cm of the compost three or four times in the growing season. If you are chive mad, cut off the flower stem before it flowers, which will divert the plant's energy to producing more leaves.

Chives are a hardy perennial, which means that they will die down at the end of the growing season and come back next year, but only if you allow the last crop of leaves to photosynthesise and feed the bulb for next year. This means letting the leaves die down naturally, as you would for a daffodil or a snowdrop. For more on bulbs, see page 157.

TO EAT   I cut chives into creamed butter in vast quantities for emerald-speckled, onion-scented fat with which to anoint all manner of cooked vegetables. If you cut too many you can also freeze the clippings in ice cubes and melt them one by one whenever you want. The flowers are beauteous, not just eaten in salad but also displayed in little vases with other summer bounty.

AND MORE   You can force chives in winter by digging up a few, re-potting them in a small pot with multi-purpose compost and putting the pot inside by a window.

Windowsill herbs

Before I was armed with any basic information about plants, I used to go through a yearly ritual of planting up a window box with all the herbs I fancied, thinking I'd have fresh produce at my fingertips for ever and ever, and then getting cross and put off when some of them died on me, as they always did. Being a little slow on the uptake in most things and having a memory like a sieve didn't improve matters, and consequently growing herbs got relegated to the bursting box inside my head labelled 'things which are difficult'. Actually, all I needed was one piece of information …

THE LOWDOWN

The thing to know about culinary herbs is that some are perennial and some are annual. This means that some will be permanent fixtures in the container and others will die at the end of the season. All you need to do is separate them. The following is my suggestion for how to have all the basic herbs you need for a Jamie Oliver supper at your fingertips. I suggest the size of the pot and the type of compost, together with watering and feeding requirements. Pick and choose the plant as you please – bearing in mind that you may need more than one windowsill.

TIMING

Pot up herbs in spring when they are growing vigorously.

HERBS YOU CAN PLANT TOGETHER

Bay (*Laurus nobilis*); Rosemary (*Rosmarinus*); Sage (*Salvia*) A basic triumvirate of pretty much evergreen herbs. Use a window box as large as your windowsill and a mixture of two-thirds multi-purpose compost and one-third grit. Arrange the plants how you want, remembering that this is a permanent thing and therefore may as well be decorative. Don't over-water – all these herbs like to be on the dry side. Keep them in shape by harvesting regularly.

HERBS BEST PLANTED IN THEIR OWN POT

Mint (*Mentha*); Thyme (*Thymus*); Chives (*Allium schoenoprasum*) I have loads of different varieties of mint and thyme all over the place, and I grow chives on my kitchen windowsill (see recipes on pages 82, 27 and 85). **Oregano or wild marjoram (*Origanum*)** There are lots of different forms. Whichever you choose, plant it in a pot slightly larger than the one it's sold in so it can spread (mine is overflowing out of a 30cm pot). Use two-thirds multi-purpose compost with one-third grit. Water sparingly. Feed with liquid seaweed after flowering, cutting the plant to within 6–7cm of the soil. It will come back next spring.

ANNUAL HERBS

Buy these in little pots in spring and summer from a garden centre (not a supermarket: the herbs for sale there are usually seedlings and need separating before potting on – see Supermarket basil, page 88). Put them in their own pots, slightly larger than the ones they were sold in. Some will keep going for longer than others, but eventually you'll want to chuck them out and get new ones the next year. You will never need to buy outrageously priced cut herbs in the supermarket again. Requirements are listed next to each entry.

Basil (*Ocimum basilicum*) See the recipe on page 88.

Chervil (*Anthriscus cerefolium*) Semi-shade. Multi-purpose compost, no grit. Don't let it dry out.

Coriander (*Coriandrum sativum*) This is not the best herb to grow if you are short on space, as it grows too high to have on a windowsill and needs staking. It also smells rank until it matures, so perhaps leave that one to the experts.

Dill (*Anethum graveolens*) Full sun. Multi-purpose compost and a handful of grit. Better grown on the ground than a windowsill, as it needs staking to stop it flopping over, but worth it if a windowsill is all you have because it's so delicious.

Parsley (*Petroselinum crispum*) Actually a hardy biennial, but I just buy a pot every year. Parsley is a greedy plant and likes to be looked after. Use multi-purpose compost mixed half and half with John Innes No. 2 and keep it well watered. Keep cutting it to encourage new growth and feed it weekly with liquid seaweed.

Supermarket basil

Everyone who keeps plants has one particular thing that they try and fail with time and time again. Mine is basil. So far my efforts at growing it from seed and keeping it alive and productive have been pretty unsuccessful. This is a delicate plant, and perhaps I do not give it the attention it needs; at any rate, it seems to keep dying on me. The sense of loss is always more keenly felt when one has invested time and energy in nurturing something from seed, so now I keep myself in basil by using this supermarket technique taught to me by an experienced gardener of many years. The plant still dies, but it gives me a continuous crop over two months or so, which is a vast improvement on what I had before.

THE LOWDOWN Basil (*Ocimum basilicum*) is an annual, or sometimes perennial, but only when it is planted in conditions akin to those of its original home of tropical or subtropical Asia. There and in the Mediterranean it occupies a habitat that the books call 'hot, dry scrub', but if you ask me, that's rather misleading – the sort of phrase I would (gleefully) associate with not having to water too much. Nothing could be further from the truth. Although basil will produce its aromatic essential oil in direct correlation to the amount of sun it gets, it's important to remember that if the plant is to have a chance of doing any of this, these hot, sunny conditions must be offset by moist fertile soil. This is worth remembering for any plant that does something like producing knock-out aromas and big leaves: the energy has to come from somewhere.

TIMING Basil's natural growing time is in summer, so starting this project in July is more likely to produce encouraging results.

YOU WILL NEED **1 large pot of growing basil** From a supermarket.
3 small terracotta pots Of course you can use any old pots, but these are going to be on your windowsill (probably in your kitchen) for a while, so it's important to help them look as gorgeous as possible. Mine are 8cm diameter.
Ordinary multi-purpose compost

METHOD Remove the plant from its plastic pot. You will see that this is actually not one plant but about 50 separate ones, all crammed in like people on the tube. Plants need more space than this – that's why shunted together in this way they all die pretty fast.

Now carefully split the compost containing the basil into two halves. Take the first half and split it in half again. Take one of the quarters and divide it into four clumps containing three or four plants each, and pot these clumps around the edge of a new pot, filling in the spaces with compost. Do the same in the second pot with the second plant quarter. Then take the remaining half and split it in two, putting these two halves back in opposite sides of the third pot. You now have three pots of basil. Water them well and leave them for a week to get over their feet being meddled with.

Make sure you place basil on your sunniest windowsill – the sun will improve the flavour. Start picking from the bushiest pot, always picking from above a sideshoot, so that the plant can re-grow. When you've had your fill from the first pot, the second one should have bulked up and be ready to pick from, and by the time you've finished with the third pot, the first one should have had time to recover. It's really important to water basil every day or at least every other day: you have no chance of getting lovely floppy leaves without doing your bit.

It's possible to keep these little pots growing for months, and for me the satisfaction of giving those ridiculously squashed seedlings some space to breathe is equalled (if not eclipsed) by the idea of clawing back the 79p I paid for the thing, and then some … Well, every little helps.

A cascading pot of edible flowers

If you've ever pushed your nose into a big scented cabbagey rose and been overcome with the desire to wrap your chops around it, the good news is you can, as long as that rose hasn't been sprayed with any nasty chemicals. The list of edible flowers is long and (to me) deeply exciting, as it combines two of the best things in life: flowers and food. A salad speckled with a handful of peppery-tasting blooms is a beautiful thing, and a perfect way to show off. Every edible flower has its own distinctive taste and is packed with nutrients too; and of course, the flowers feed your soul as well as your body. Begin with nasturtiums.

THE LOWDOWN
A nasturtium (*Tropaeolum majus*) is a perennial climber from Central or South America, which means that it won't abide any frost, and is therefore grown in this country as an annual. You can buy plants in the shops, but it's much cheaper and more satisfying to buy a packet of seeds, because when it comes to care, all they need is water. As with many plants grown for their flowers, the principle of 'treat them mean, keep them keen' applies: in other words, you'll get more flowers if you give them a growing medium that is on the poor side.

TIMING
Sow the seeds in March or April.

YOU WILL NEED
Nasturtium seeds Snap up a packet or two – they're widely available – and don't be a colour snob – the brighter the better. The seed companies have created lots of great mixtures. I like one called 'Little Gem Mix', which has flowers that are yellow and pillar-box red with crazy flame-like markings on some of the petals, and 'Alaska Series', which has speckled yellow and orange flowers, but if you must be tasteful and muted then the dark mahogany of 'Black Velvet' or pale yellow 'Peach Melba' are for you.
Pots, window boxes or hanging baskets *Tropaeolum* like to trail around the place, so hanging baskets or window boxes, or a pot hung on a wall, are best. Pots and baskets should be spacious enough: bear in mind that these plants like to be about 25cm from their neighbour, which means three plants to a standard hanging basket of around 35cm diameter.
Compost I use John Innes No. 2 with added horticultural grit for window boxes, and a mixture of multi-purpose compost and grit for anything I'm hanging up, in order to keep things as light as possible.
A sunny site

METHOD
Fill your containers with compost and push each seed in about 1.5cm deep and 12cm apart. This means that you're sowing more seeds than you will finally want, but acts as an insurance policy against non-germination or bird/squirrel-related disaster. Cover them up with compost and water the whole thing well until you can see water coming out of the bottom of the container. Then put the containers outside where you want them and wait patiently for a couple of weeks until seedlings appear.

Let them grow for a couple more weeks, keeping the compost nice and moist, and then gently pull out half of the seedlings so that you get a final spacing of 25cm. Thinning like this always seems like murder (and it is), but you'll get better plants if you give them the space they need. Your only job now is to keep the thing watered (nasturtiums won't perform for you if you let them dry out). You'll end up with cascading torrents of outrageous blooms which you can pluck off, wash and decorate your food with.

Nasturtiums often get attacked by blackfly and caterpillars (which is why vegetable growers often use them in between their crops). Don't be discouraged if this happens: it's a common thing and can be controlled by squishing them with your fingers or spraying them off with a jet of water. Alternatively there are various organic pesticides on the market that are safe for use on edible crops (see page 239). The trick here is to watch carefully and take action as soon as you see the critters, rather than waiting for things to get out of control.

AND MORE   Other easy-to-grow plants that have edible flowers include most culinary herbs, marigolds, lavender, violets and pansies, scented pelargoniums and day lilies. See also Borage for ice and fireworks, page 134.

Sprouting

It took me a while to 'get' the whole idea of bean sprouts, inextricably linked as they were, in my mind, with stir-fry (too much chopping) and that inexplicable vegetable called baby corn, which I loathe and detest; but Father Christmas had other ideas and I started my first packet of bean sprouts one lazy Boxing Day and have never looked back. Bean sprouts are extremely rich in minerals, protein and vitamins and therefore deeply virtuous – something that will appeal to all virgins.

THE LOWDOWN

You can buy packets of beans or seeds especially for sprouting in the seed section of garden centres; they come in single and mixed packets. Or you can go out and get your preferred seed, nut, bean or grain at an organic shop (remember that you're going to be eating a raw product and you want to make sure it's fit for the temple that is your body – and that means making sure it's free of any chemicals). The possibilities are endless when it comes to what you can sprout (see overleaf for other suggestions), but the best and most readily available material for a sprouting virgin is *Phaseolus aureus*, otherwise known as the mung bean.

TIMING

Absolutely any time – this is indoor gardening at its most convenient. You don't even need any light, so it's a perfect activity for the depths of winter.

YOU WILL NEED

Some organic mung beans See above.
A biggish jam jar
A piece of muslin
An elastic band

METHOD

Start with about 2 tablespoons of beans inside the jam jar, fill the jar up with water and give it a shake to clean the beans. Strain them through a sieve and put them back in the jar, filled with more water. Leave them to soak for 24 hours, after which they will have swollen and some of them will have begun to pop out of their little green jackets.

Place the square of muslin over the top of the jar and secure with the elastic band, and then drain all the water through the muslin. Fill the jar with water once again and shake the beans to clean them. Drain again and lay the jar on its side in a warm place (I use the space under my sink, other people put paper bags over the jars – anything to keep out the light). Repeat this washing process every day, twice a day.

The sprouting should start on day two or three. You'll see a little white tusk peeping out of the split green jacket. You can start eating the sprouted beans now if you want, or at any time until their leaves appear, which will be on about day seven. Bear in mind that the sprouts you produce in this way are never going to look like commercially produced ones, which are sprouted under pressure (and this is perfectly possible to do at home too, if you decide that sprouting is your thing).

You can do masses with bean sprouts, but I like to sprinkle them on salads. I have also found them to be a thing of joy for size-zero skinnies who work hard at being thin and want to stay that way: they plunge, gannet-like, into a bowl of these with the same zeal that I reserve strictly for treacle tart and custard – but each to her own.

AND MORE   Other things to sprout include adzuki beans, alfalfa seeds (the most nutritious of all seeds), almonds (skin on), chickpeas, fenugreek, maize, millet, oats, pumpkin seeds, quinoa, rice, sesame seeds and loads more. If you develop a penchant for this sort of thing, this is just the beginning: a wheatgrass lawn and indoor salads (see page 95) are your next step – the sprouting equivalent of second base.

Salad leaves for year-round rabbit food

There are manifold ways of growing salad leaves on the kitchen windowsill to provide you with lovely fresh rabbit food throughout the growing season. Most of these complicated permutations come down to what you choose to grow, though, which is why a packet of mixed salad seeds is such a godsend to a virgin like me. Buying salad in plastic bags will seem like madness when you realise how easy it is to grow your own, and it is perfectly possible to remove the need for this if you are organised enough about sowing new seeds every couple of weeks or so. I am not, and consequently I tend to occupy a middle ground in which I supplement what I buy with what I grow — after all, what on earth is the point of being virtuous if you are stressed out into the bargain?

THE LOWDOWN
Growers of vegetables call this method of growing leaves 'cut-and-come-again', because it works on the principle that when they're young, lots of leafy things will take another crack at growth after they've been chopped. Sometimes they'll do this two or three times, providing a continual supply of young leaves for us to munch.

The people at the seed companies have devoted their time and energy to providing us with mixtures that will grow well together — with names like 'Saladini', 'Saladisi', 'Mesclun' or 'Niche' — which will give you salad leaves from spring to autumn for less than the cost of a bag of supermarket salad; what's not to like? The other thing is that you can grow this stuff indoors in a light place throughout the winter too.

TIMING
Any time between spring and autumn, but if it's your first time, do this in spring.

YOU WILL NEED
A packet of mixed salad seeds Buy these from the garden centre or a supermarket.
A seed tray Any old plastic carton will do, but make sure it has holes in the bottom for drainage and will fit on your windowsill. I used to use old ice-cream tubs but have graduated to using larger seed trays, 38cm by 24cm, which are sturdier and have greater surface area for more leaves. Round shallow terracotta pots are lovely too, especially for bringing to the table.
Multi-purpose compost

METHOD
Fill the container with compost and drop it on to a hard surface a couple of times from a height of a few centimetres to settle the contents and make a nice firm bed for the seeds. Then scatter the seeds very thinly on the surface and cover them gently with about 1cm or so of compost. Water the whole thing carefully with the rose of a watering can or by placing the tray in another tray of water for a couple of hours until the whole thing is glistening with moisture. Put the tray outside on a sunny windowsill and keep an eye on it to make sure it doesn't dry out.

Depending on what your seed mixture contains, the seeds will germinate in anything from a few days to three weeks. I often indulge in a bit of surgery when the shoots appear, pulling out the ones that are growing very close together, so that each shoot has a couple of centimetres around it, but this is not strictly necessary.

The first batch of salad will be ready a few weeks after that. Always cut or pinch the leaves off from a point just above either the seed leaves (first leaves) or the first pair of true leaves, in order for the seedling to begin growing again. I frequently bring the whole thing to the table so that people can pick their own.

The range of intensity in flavour is fascinating, so it really is worth tasting your seedlings every few days to find out when they are most delicious. If you love them very, very young then you are deeply trendy – these are micro-greens, and utterly in vogue.

Cherry tomatoes

One perfect mouthful, one slow squeeze … one sweet explosion inside the mouth. I know everyone says it, but a tomato tastes even better if it's home-grown. I grow one or two plants inside my kitchen window, where they're easy to get at every time I need a fix.

THE LOWDOWN The tomato (*Lycopersicon esculentum*) is a tender annual from South America and comes in many, many permutations. You can grow tomatoes from seed really easily, but for this first foray into tomatoland it's best to buy small plants from a garden centre. Good reliable varieties of cherry tomatoes include 'Sakura', which has a high yield, 'Red Cherry' or 'Sweet Olive' for sweetness, and the ever-wonderful 'Gardener's Delight', which totally lives up to its name and is the one you're most likely to find at the garden centre.

TIMING Tomato plants are available from around April. Buy one as soon as you see them.

YOU WILL NEED **1 young tomato plant** See above.
A pot about 20cm in diameter
Multi-purpose compost
1 bamboo cane about 1.5m long or taller
A bottle of liquid tomato food Available at garden centres in a red bottle.

METHOD Take your young tomato out of its plastic pot and plant it in its new one, firming the compost gently around it, and stick the cane in the edge of the pot (taking care not to damage the roots), ready for the tomato plant to be tethered to. Water the plant in well and put the pot by a sunny window with a saucer underneath it to collect any stray water. Keep the compost damp and feed the plant once a week from the red bottle, following the instructions to the letter. Tomatoes should appear from about mid-July onwards. Eat them one by one, as they ripen, bearing in mind that you do not have to share.

AND MORE To maximise your crop you can do the following:

❊ Train your plant into a cordon (one stem only) by pinching out all the sideshoots. These are the shoots that form at the axis of the leaf and the main stem. Don't confuse them with flower trusses, which grow directly from the stem between the leaves.

❊ In late August, or when it's got to the top of its cane support, pinch out the top of the main stem. This is called 'stopping' and will make the plant divert all its energy to ripening the fruits.

❊ Pinch off the older leaves at the base of the plant to increase airflow and allow light to reach the ripening fruit.

Peter Rabbit carrots

This is the only way you'll get me to eat a raw carrot — enormous, watery supermarket carrots are good for one thing only, and that's buried inside a carrot cake. Growing your own baby carrots in pots is embarrassingly easy, and you can get delicious, really yummy, proper, finger-sized roots complete with greenery in August — the sort they serve in really posh restaurants — and keep on harvesting them well into autumn.

THE LOWDOWN
Peter Rabbit's favourite vegetable is a taproot — a storage organ for the plant where it keeps all the sugars it needs in order to grow. It's a biennial (flowering in its second year to produce seed), and has been bred into loads of different shapes and sizes. Its wild parent, *Daucus carota*, hails from Europe and South-western Asia.

TIMING
Start at the end of April or beginning of May.

YOU WILL NEED
Carrot seed Available at garden centres and even supermarkets. The best for this project are 'Primo', which gives a good yield, 'Early Nantes', an old variety for the nostalgic in me, and 'Parmex', which are spherical, like a cherry tomato, and perfect for a shallower pot. All these taste a world away from anything you can buy in the shops.
Containers You'll want two at least, so that you can get early carrots from one and let the other one grow on for later nibblings. I use terracotta because it's prettier, but plastic is easier as it retains water better. Whichever you choose, make sure it is about 30cm in diameter and has a capacity of at least 10 litres — remember that your carrots need space to grow down.
Multi-purpose compost
A sunny site

METHOD
Fill the pots with compost and tap them once or twice on the ground to settle it in. Scatter the seed thinly (about 1cm apart) on the surface and sprinkle more compost on top, just to cover lightly. Then water the whole thing well with the fine rose of a watering can and wait patiently. Keep the pot outdoors in a sunny site, just moist, not wet — carrots don't like it wet.

The first morsels will be ready for pulling in early August. I serve them in their virgin state — just pulled, dirt washed off and with their greenery intact — piled on a plate in the middle of the table for people to grab and munch.

AND MORE
If you can bear to sacrifice yield for aesthetics, you should mix some feathery-leaved annuals, such as love-in-a-mist (*Nigella damascena*) or cornflower (*Centaurea cyanus*) in with your carrot seed. This will not only add to the gorgeosity of the carrot foliage but also deter and confuse the dreaded carrot fly (which, at any rate, is not nearly so much of a problem with pot-grown carrots as it is with carrots grown in the ground).

Strawberries

Strawberries are edible plants that also have stand-alone ornamental magic – and doubly so if you plant them in hanging baskets. I have never got along with those special strawberry pots with holes in the sides, and I find hanging baskets altogether more appealing, as the fruit is at nose height. The other advantage of growing in hanging baskets instead of in (or near) the ground is that the fruit is protected from slimy invertebrates (whose tastes are alarmingly similar to our own), and there is no need to lay straw or other material under the fruits to stop them rotting from contact with the soil.

THE LOWDOWN

Strawberries belong to the *Rosaceae* family; look at the flowers and you will notice the similarity to wild roses. They are perennials and come from open woodland, grassy places and hedgerows all over Europe, Asia and North America, so they need full sun or dappled shade, and fertile soil. Strawberries grown for their fruit fall into four categories: early, mid-season, late-season and perpetual. The name of the category refers to time of fruiting, with perpetual varieties fruiting in both summer and autumn. I use the early varieties 'Rosie' and 'Honeoye' or mid-season 'Hapil' because I get rather sick of strawberries after July. My favourite strawberry for texture and flavour is one called 'Elsanta'. There are people who specialise in strawberry plants, but I have always bought mine from my local nursery.

TIMING

Spring to summer.

YOU WILL NEED

Strawberry plants Two or three small plants per basket. They appear in garden centres in spring.

Hanging basket There are so many different ones to choose from, but the basic rule here is that you get what you pay for. Buy a cheap, pre-lined one this year and then decide whether you enjoy using it enough to invest a bit more time and energy into something more permanent. The important thing is that the lining needs to be porous so that excess water can get out. If the basket is lined with plastic, cut holes in it.

Compost Multi-purpose compost is best for hanging baskets, because it's loamless and therefore lighter.

Pea gravel This will aid water retention.

Tomato feed This is not just for tomatoes: it's a fertiliser containing high levels of potassium to induce flowering and fruiting. It usually comes in a red bottle.

METHOD   Fill your basket with compost and carefully plant your strawberry plants in a circle around the edge. Fill in with compost, leaving some room for watering, and cover the surface around the plants with a thin layer of pea gravel to keep it from drying out too quickly.

Hang the basket up somewhere light, and water it thoroughly so that the whole thing is soaked and water is coming out of the bottom. Keep the basket well watered – strawberries can be juicy only if they have water to create juice from, so do not let them dry out.

As soon as you see a flower, start feeding by adding a capful (follow the instructions on the bottle) of tomato feed to your watering can every ten days or so. I am not religious about this, but I'd probably get more fruit if I were. I find it's best to buy new plants each year so I can try out new varieties, and because I don't have the greenhouse to get them through the winter.

TO EAT   I often take down my baskets and put them on the table after supper with friends, shored up by an old circular cooking mould that I have (you know, one of the ones you're supposed to use to make those horrific gelatinous fish mousses), other bowls of summer fruit, lots of cream and white sugar, and let people get involved.

A gooseberry lollipop in a pot

In my humble opinion, a gooseberry is possibly the sexiest fruit on the planet: sweet, tart and juicy ... So far so obvious, but then there's an unassuming, laid-back quality to a gooseberry that makes it attractive — and all the more so because its looks give little indication as to just how exquisite it is. Add to this the plum-like, veiny translucency of the thing, and the spiky hairiness of some gooseberries, and biting into this fruit becomes deliciously, naughtily obscene ... But perhaps I should get out more.

My mother (famed for many things but not her culinary skills) used to serve gooseberry fool regularly — a great, great pudding indeed, and something for which your harvest does not have to be the embodiment of perfection.

I suggest using a standard lollipop plant here, in accordance with my need for things to be beautiful as well as useful. It's more expensive but worth it, particularly in a small space. However, the method and size of container below will work for a bush too.

THE LOWDOWN — People used to serve gooseberries (*Ribes uva-crispa*) with roast goose — hence the name. They are the first soft fruit to be ready (in May time) and if a plastic carton of them from the supermarket doesn't do it for you, and you have the outside space, they are easy-peasy to grow. Gooseberries are very hardy.

TIMING — Plant gooseberries in autumn or spring.

YOU WILL NEED — **A standard gooseberry bush** Either buy them from a specialist nursery (see Suppliers, page 262), who can advise on which variety would be best, or you may find one or be able to order it from some of the larger garden centres. Good reliable varieties include 'Greenfinch', 'Invicta' (green-berried), 'Pax' and 'Rokula' (red). Your plant may well be sold 'bare-root' (i.e. with no soil or pot). They are sold like this in order to keep costs down, and must be planted quickly.

A spot that's sunny or only partially shaded, and, if possible, sheltered Although a gooseberry is pretty good at dealing with most conditions. The only thing it must have is enough water.

Containers Your gooseberry will eventually need a large container like a half-barrel (about 50cm x 40cm), but you will need to work up to this, starting with a pot slightly larger than the one it is in, or one with a 30cm diameter if it's bare-root. You will then increase the size of the container every spring until it goes into its final pot. This will take three to four years.

Compost Use John Innes No. 3.

A handful of Osmacote granules (See page 229.)

METHOD   If you are planting in the ground, you need to prepare it a month or two before you plant your gooseberry. Remove all weeds and dig a square hole about 50cm wide and about a spade's depth deep. Now chuck in some well-rotted manure or garden compost to enrich the soil, work it in with a fork, and then cover it with the soil you removed.

If your plant comes in a pot, plant it, making sure it is at the same depth in its new home as it was in its pot. To plant a bare-root specimen, the depth should be obvious on the main stem where there will be a clear line of dirt to guide you in your planting. Make sure all the roots are in contact with the soil or compost by creating a mound in the planting hole and spreading the bare roots over it before covering with soil or compost (see page 120 for more information). As you do this, keep hold of the stem of the plant, and agitate it a little so that the crumbs of soil or compost can fall into the gaps between the roots. Firm the plant in well and water it in properly.

Pruning is easy for a standard: just cut away errant shoots in winter to maintain the lollipop shape. If you have a bush then the supplier should provide you with pruning instructions to maintain the all-important 'open-goblet' shape that will produce the most fruit.

You can (and should) start picking gooseberries from mid-May to early June. This fruit will be semi-ripe and if you pick every other berry you can make gooseberry fool with these and leave the rest to grow plump and sweet.

TO EAT   Here is my mother's recipe for gooseberry fool. Place **gooseberries** in a pan with **granulated sugar** to taste and cook down to a pulp. Put it through a sieve or mouli and add plenty of **whipped cream**. Mix them up and sprinkle **toasted almonds** on top and serve the fool cold from the fridge.

Redcurrants for jelly

I never pass up an opportunity to get geeky in the kitchen, and although making jams and jellies is hardly rocket science, I still get a slight frisson in the presence of ... well, pectin. Redcurrants are fabulously high in pectin, and wonderfully obliging plants too.

THE LOWDOWN
Redcurrants (*Ribes rubrum*) are deciduous shrubs from western Europe. Birds love them, but if you're suitably vigilant you'll still get enough from one bush to make jelly. You can buy them trained as cordons (plants pruned so that they look like Is, Us or Ws and terribly smart) or fans. (See Suppliers, page 262.) The supplier should give you pruning instructions, and if they don't, ask for them. Redcurrants are unfussy about soil and aspect as long as they get enough water.

TIMING
For instant gratification spring is best.

YOU WILL NEED
1 redcurrant plant Trained as a cordon (see above).
Wire and vine eyes
Well-prepared ground See page 105.
Soft twine

METHOD
Prepare a wall first, by attaching some supports such as lines of wire attached with vine eyes. This is boring but well worth it, because this plant is shallow rooting and doesn't like being buffeted about in the wind. Plant your cordon in well-prepared ground and attach it gently to the wires, using soft twine.

Your redcurrant will need feeding every March with a general fertiliser such as Growmore, a mulch of well-rotted manure or garden compost on top of this, and a regular supply of water. It will start producing currants around July (hang an inconspicuous net over them if need be). Pick them as soon as they ripen.

TO EAT
Here is a recipe for redcurrant jelly from the glorious Prue Leith. Place all the **redcurrants** you can pick, rinsed, into an earthenware dish. Put this in the oven at 180°C/gas mark 4 for about an hour until the juice has run out of the redcurrants, mashing them a few times as they cook. Strain through clean muslin and leave overnight to drain.

Next day put a saucer into your freezer, and prepare some jars by running them through the dishwasher, drying them thoroughly and putting them in the oven on a low heat. Measure the juice and pour it into a saucepan with **450g granulated sugar** to every 570ml of juice. Dissolve the sugar over a low heat and then bring it to the boil. After five minutes remove the pan from the heat, put a teaspoon of the liquid on to your freezing saucer and return it to the freezer for a minute or two until the liquid is cold. Push the liquid with your finger and if it has a wrinkly skin, it's done. If not, continue to boil and test.

Pour the jelly into the warmed jars and seal each one with a circle of waxed paper and cover with a circle of cellophane, brushing it with water so that it stretches tightly over the top. Secure with an elastic band.

Raspberries

A bumptious raspberry pyramid will give you fresh fruit and something structurally appealing with which to adorn your outside space, whether it's a back yard or a balcony; and purchasing raspberry canes will be rather more fruitful than haemorrhaging money on topiary. I describe here how to grow raspberries in a container, but you can of course plant the canes in the ground instead.

THE LOWDOWN

Raspberries belong to the genus *Rubus* – all are prickly plants and extremely tough. They come from a range of habitats worldwide. The species we eat is called *R. idaeus*, and it's best to start with an autumn-fruiting cultivar called 'Autumn Bliss'. You'll get fruit from August to October, and there's nothing nicer when the year is beginning to wane. The other great thing about this raspberry, especially if you are planting it in the ground, is that it is self-supporting, so you don't have to spend your precious time erecting supports if that's not your thing. Raspberries are sold as canes, either bare-rooted or in pots, and because 'Autumn Bliss' is so popular it's easy to find in garden centres.

TIMING

You can plant pot-grown raspberries at any time, but a spring planting will give you fruit in the same year.

YOU WILL NEED

5 canes of 'Autumn Bliss' raspberry Available from most garden centres or online.

A big pot I suggest a half-barrel, about 80cm in diameter and lined with plastic. If you can't find a lined one, you can do it yourself with a sheet of black plastic and a staple-gun.

Some bricks

A bag of gravel

John Innes No. 3 compost This is best for fruit.

5 bamboo canes These need to be 2.4m long.

A sunny site Although, being derived from woodland plants, a little shade is fine.

METHOD

First make sure your barrel and the plastic lining have holes in them for drainage. Now decide where you want to grow your raspberries, bearing in mind that moving this pot will not be much of an option once it is full. Arrange the bricks in a circle and put the barrel on top, so that it's raised off the ground, and then put a layer of gravel in the bottom to prevent the drainage holes from blocking.

Fill the barrel with compost so that when you place the raspberries in their pots on it there is a good 7–10cm between the rims of the pots and the top of the barrel. Arrange them in a circle inside the barrel, still in their pots, and fill in all the gaps with more compost, firming it gently down. Now extract the raspberries in their pots, so that you are left with five perfectly shaped holes in the compost. Discard the plastic pots, and put the raspberry canes back in the holes. Firm the compost around the plants, adding more if necessary, and stick a bamboo cane next to each plant, being careful not to stab the roots. Plunge each cane right down to the bottom of the barrel so that it's firmly in place. Then bring the tops of the canes together to make a wigwam and tie with string.

Lastly, tie each raspberry cane to its support and water the barrel until you can see it dripping out of the bottom. It's a good idea to put gravel over the top of the compost around the plants, to help retain moisture.

By summertime you will have a beautiful lime-green pyramid, and fruit will start appearing in August.

You should prune the canes right down to the base in February, and feed your raspberries with something like Growmore (a liquid solution is best for a pot) in March so that they can do it all over again. Keep a lookout for pests such as raspberry beetles; these can be controlled with an organic pesticide (see page 239). Birds love raspberries too, and if you don't want to share, you might wish to cover your wigwam with some netting to keep them from stealing.

AND MORE   Raspberries are best when they're fed to you, one by one, by someone other than yourself.

Blueberries for muffin-lovers

A home-grown blueberry is a beautiful thing, and so is a muffin (of any description). The two together produce something close to sublime. Blueberries are easy to grow and extremely pretty in their own right: they burst into pink blossom in the spring and have intoxicating autumn colour.

THE LOWDOWN
Highbush blueberries, like cranberries and bilberries, belong to the genus *Vaccinium*. They are also known as heathland berries (belonging, as they do, to the heather family), and originate from eastern North America. They are deciduous shrubs and perfectly hardy in the UK. Because they are so utterly delicious and health-giving, much work has been done on them by clever people, yielding a plethora of cultivars. They are usually sold in pairs or threes, because to set fruit, the flowers need pollinating; so if you're buying plants separately, make sure their flowering times overlap. The only other stipulation is that they must have an acidic soil, and that means a pH (see page 228) of between 4 and 5, so if you don't have an outside space where rhododendrons and azaleas grow really well (this is the marker of good acid soil), grow them in containers.

TIMING
It's best to plant blueberries in containers in the springtime. If you're planting them in the ground, though, do so between November and March (i.e. after the leaves have fallen).

YOU WILL NEED
2 or 3 blueberry plants of different varieties Either order these from a specialist grower who can advise you, or go to a good nursery and pick up a pack of two or three (see above).
Crocks or broken-up polystyrene To provide good drainage.
Containers at least 35cm in diameter One for each plant.
Ericaceous compost You can buy this in bags.
Bark chippings or leafmould For leafmould, see page 162.
A patio or balcony in full sun or partial shade

METHOD
For each plant, put a layer of crocks or broken-up polystyrene in the bottom of the pot and plant your blueberry so that the top of the compost is at the same level that it was in its original pot, allowing a gap of 3cm or so at the top so when you water it you don't produce a flood. I cover the top of the compost with a layer of bark chippings as a mulch in order to conserve moisture, but it would be even better if you used leafmould.

Water the whole thing thoroughly with rainwater or filtered water (both of which are softer – i.e. have less lime – than tap water), until you can see the water coming out of the bottom of the container. It's really important to keep the plant moist by watering little and often. Tap water is better than nothing in an emergency, but rainwater or filtered water is essential to the long-term health of the plant.

I feed my pots with an ericaceous liquid fertiliser once a fortnight (when my brain remembers) while they're growing between spring and autumn. There will be two flushes of growth. The first flowers will arrive at the ends of the branches that grew in the previous season, and then in summer, new shoots should appear from the base of the plant, with more flowers and (usually juicier) fruit. Don't prune your bush for the first three years while it gets established, except to cut out any dead or diseased stems and generally keep it looking nice. After this you can get a bit more technical about pruning (see page 232).

TO EAT After eating blueberries au naturel in great fistfuls, blueberry muffins are the next best thing. They must be proper, American massive ones, like those you get in diners, for which you will need a six-cup jumbo muffin tin.

I most often use a muffin mix from the supermarket, but if you want to make them from scratch, toss **2 handfuls blueberries** in **1 tablespoon flour** and use a large mixing bowl to combine **240g flour, 130g granulated sugar, 2 teaspoons baking powder, ¼ teaspoon baking soda** and a **good pinch of salt**. Whisk together **1 large egg** and **250ml buttermilk** with **1 teaspoon vanilla extract** and **6 tablespoons melted butter** (cooled) and pour them in the centre of the dry ingredients, combining them gradually and gently, and finally adding the blueberries (again, gently) so that you have gorgeous lumpy batter.

Butter the muffin tin generously, or use paper muffin cases, and spoon in the batter; then cook in a pre-heated oven at 180°C/gas mark 4 for half an hour or so until a toothpick comes out clean. Eat with a long glass of cold milk.

Broad beans

If I found myself plonked on a desert island or death row, a bowl of steamed broad beans, slipped out of their skins, served with olive oil and lemon, would be just fine.

THE LOWDOWN

There's evidence that people have been growing broad beans (or fava beans) to eat since 6000 BC, so it's an ancient crop; and they are full of all sorts of good things like L-dopa, which is used to treat Parkinson's and low libido, amongst other things. The broad bean plant is tall and erect, sometimes reaching 2m high, and fully hardy. The Latin name is *Vicia faba* and it originates from North Africa. Fresh, bright-green broad beans are very special, and the plant itself is beautiful, each flower having two black spots (very distinguished), which means that even if you don't have space outside for a crop of these, it's still worth growing just one in a pot. Instead of growing from seed, as I describe here, you could buy young plants.

TIMING

Sow your beans between February and April.

YOU WILL NEED

A packet of broad bean seeds Available from garden centres.
Root trainers or little pots inside a tray with a plastic lid (Optional.)
Gritty seed-compost (Optional.)
Some well-dug soil in a sunny sheltered site If your soil is heavy, add some grit for drainage: wetness will rot the seeds.
Bamboo canes
String

METHOD

Either sow your beans directly into the soil in rows, spacing them 20cm apart, or do as I do and start them off on a windowsill in root trainers filled with seed compost (see page 21). This way you can watch them and they're less likely to rot. Push the seeds in 5cm deep, water them well and in about three weeks they'll have burst out of the ground.

If you've sown them in situ, you'll just need to watch them grow. If they've been started off elsewhere, plant them out in the ground. Either way, unless you've bought a dwarf variety, they'll need some support, and for this I just put a pair of bamboo canes at the end of each row and tie string to them so that the plants can grow up through the middle.

You'll have a bowl of beans in less than two months. Blackfly love the young shoots so control the pests by pinching out the tips of the plants when they start to flower and spraying them with an organic pesticide (see page 239).

TO EAT

Steam your beans and squeeze each one out of its skin. They taste far more delicious like this – I think it has something to do with the small extra effort involved – and of course the colour is just magical. They are wonderful in a risotto with asparagus, too; or you could, of course, team them up with liver and a nice Chianti …

Growing garlic

Being a relatively expensive kitchen staple and ridiculously easy to grow yourself, growing garlic is doubly satisfying. (NB always share garlic … People know if you've been selfish.)

THE LOWDOWN *Allium sativum* is a bulbous plant and comes from the onion family (*Alliaceae*). It originates from dry and mountainous areas, probably in Central Asia. The plant has grey-green leaves and umbels of bell-shaped white flowers in summer. There are two distinct types of garlic for growing, hardneck and softneck. I like hardneck because it has bigger bulbs that are easier to peel. Softneck is generally what you will find in the supermarket, as it has a longer shelf life. You can tell the difference by feeling the central stalk: softneck is papery, hardneck is rigid, like a pencil.

TIMING Late autumn / early winter (October to February, depending on your area). Garlic needs a cold period of at least a month before the weather warms up in order for bulbs to form.

YOU WILL NEED **Garlic** While it is perfectly possible to grow garlic using cloves from your local supermarket, you will get a better result if you buy fresh garlic from someone who grows it themselves, to ensure it is disease-free and exactly what you want. For this, go to a local farmers' market, where a stallholder will be able to tell you all about different varieties, or to one of those posh organic supermarkets who buy from small growers. Alternatively, you can order garlic from one of the suppliers I have listed on page 262. Most importantly, decide whether you like it before you grow it.
A sunny place You can use either an open site in the garden or a container somewhere south-facing.
Well-drained soil Dry, mountainous areas are rocky, so add grit if your soil is very heavy. In a container, use a half-and-half mixture of multi-purpose and John Innes No. 2, with a few handfuls of added grit.

METHOD Separate the largest cloves from each bulb (these are usually those around the outside), and make sure each clove has its own piece of basal plate (the flat bit at the bottom). Push the cloves about 5cm deep into the soil, pointed side up and 15cm apart, and cover them up with soil. Give them a label, and some water if the soil is very dry.

Shoots will appear in early spring and the plant will be about 60cm high by late spring. Dig the garlic up when the leaves start to go brown, being careful not to damage the bulbs. You can start eating immediately, but be sure to hang some of them up so that the sap can travel down into the bulbs and swell them (what you are doing here is effectively curing them, like meat, so the flavour becomes more intense with time). The bulbs will keep for several months in the kitchen, provided they are stored somewhere well ventilated.

TO EAT   I use my first harvest as the star of the show by cutting entire bulbs in half horizontally and putting them in the oven in foil pouches with olive oil, so that they half roast, half steam. They go on plates in the middle of the table with good white bread, olive oil and some teaspoons so that people can scoop out the sweet sticky contents.

AND MORE   The benefits of garlic are widely reported when it comes to well-being, but gardeners also use it as a natural pesticide, planting it with their precious ornamental plants to help keep pests away. Needless to say, this also works with humans.

Saffron

OK: it takes an awful lot of flowers to produce saffron in any kind of significant quantity, but they are so exquisite that it's worth growing this plant for its beauty alone. You can grow saffron crocus en masse in your garden, if you have one, or in containers, which kind of adds to this plant's general air of rarity and preciousness.

THE LOWDOWN *Crocus sativus*, the saffron crocus, is an autumn-flowering perennial that grows from a corm (like a bulb, but technically a swollen stem). It has rich purple flowers with dark blue veining, which open wide to reveal the three-branched fiery style (the female part of the flower).

This plant is very likely the result of man's breeding, though the exact origin is uncertain – it's probably from Greece. It has been cultivated by all the ancient civilisations and used as a drug, scent, dye or spice, and in the present day it grows as happily in North Wales as it does in Kashmir, so it is a very well-tempered plant and a virgin's dream. Saffron likes a relatively cushy life, somewhere nice, sheltered and sunny, with a rich soil.

TIMING Plant in summer – June, July or August.

YOU WILL NEED **Some *Crocus sativus* corms** These are beautiful, silky-hairy little things with wispy tips that look like small mouse tails. They are sold in some garden centres and to order (in winter) from bulb specialists (see Suppliers, page 262).
Containers If you're using them, make sure they are at least 25cm high (*Crocus sativus* likes to be planted deep).
Compost (If you're using containers.) I use a 50/50 mix of multi-purpose and John Innes No. 2, with a few handfuls of horticultural grit.

METHOD Whether you're planting in the ground or in pots, make sure the corms are about 15cm deep and 10cm apart, so that they can bulk up and reproduce. After an initial watering in, you can keep them dryish until September, when they'll need some water to get the roots growing strongly.

The first shoots should appear in October. If you can bear to massacre the flowers for saffron, pick them and carefully remove the stigmas, which are the long, fiery threads that form the top of the style. Leave them to dry in a warm place (away from draughts) for about a week.

When you serve food infused with your own saffron, do not be a shrinking violet: this is definitely one to brag about.

A runner bean wigwam

You can grow runner beans like this either in a pot or on a spare patch of earth. Erecting a structure like a wigwam is also a wonderful lesson in what a difference it makes to add height to a space — you don't actually have to grow anything up it at all.

THE LOWDOWN Runner beans (*Phaseolus coccineus*) are tender perennial climbers and as such are usually grown as annuals. They were originally introduced from their native Central America for their ornamental properties: they will climb up pretty much anything without any help at all, which makes them perfect for screening.

Most runner beans have scarlet flowers that have both male and female parts but need to be 'tripped' by a bee landing on the lower petals so that the stamens (the pollen-covered male parts of the flower) touch the pistil (the female bit if the flower, with its ovary containing the cells that need fertilising to make the beans). You can buy runner bean seeds or little plants (you'll need eight) in most garden centres. You can quite easily do this project in a pot (a large one) on a smaller scale with, say, three canes and three beans, using multi-purpose compost.

TIMING Start this project between May and June.

YOU WILL NEED **A packet of runner bean seeds** There are loads of different cultivars, each with their own merits – pick the one you like best. You need eight plants for one wigwam. I sow double this amount (see Method).
A piece of earth about 1m square This needs to have been dug over. Runner beans like to root deeply. The spot can be partially shaded, but it's better if it's not. If you really want a bumper harvest and you are very organised, do this the previous autumn and line the bottom of your square with some shredded newspaper or manure mixed with straw to help retain moisture before you pile the soil back on top.
8 long bamboo canes These need to be at least 2.4m high.

METHOD Push the bamboo canes well into the soil around the edge of your square metre at regular intervals. Then get someone tall or stand on a chair, and bring the top ends together and secure tightly with string.

Now sow two beans at the base of each cane, 5cm deep (or plant your young plants). Water thoroughly. When they emerge and have two lots of leaves, carefully pull out the smallest one. The beans will climb up the canes themselves without any help at all (and they will twine clockwise, by the way) and your wigwam will be covered and heaving with pretty flowers and then beans within a couple of months. The most important thing to remember is to keep the beans watered.

AND MORE Those with children could do something much larger with a couple of canes missing to create a wigwam that you can crawl inside for Hiawatha parties.

Asparagus for lovers

Growing asparagus is, like true love, a long-term project and one that needs a certain amount of commitment. Because of this, if you are ultimately prepared to share it with someone, it's a good barometer of the extent of your love. This is another crop that's really expensive to buy in the shops, and therefore it's more than worth the effort.

THE LOWDOWN

Asparagus (*Asparagus officinalis*) is a perennial plant and comes from sandy and coastal areas in Europe, Asia and Africa, so it obviously needs well-drained soil.

TIMING

Start in March.

YOU WILL NEED

Asparagus crowns These are one-year-old plants with root systems. The best thing to do is order these, and they'll be sent to you in good condition by someone who cares. At any rate, order them in time for planting in March. How many you get is dependent on how much space you are willing to give over to this project. They need to be planted roughly 30cm apart.
A weed-free, sunny site

METHOD

Dig a trench about 30cm wide and 20cm deep, leaving a ridge of soil about 8cm high running along the centre. Then carefully splay the roots of each crown out over this little hummock and cover them with about 5cm of soil. In the first year, don't cut any of the stems, and in the second year cut only one stem per crown. After three years you can start harvesting them properly, cutting all the shoots that appear until the end of spring, or June at the latest, after which you must let the rest grow into the lovely frothy ferny mass that it wants to be. This will ensure that the plant can regenerate and provide for you next year. To cut asparagus, use a sharp knife and make a clean cut about 5cm underneath the soil.

Mulch the beds with something nourishing like manure or grass clippings, but as soon as the frost has gone, rake this off so that the roots can sense that it's time to get going again.

The initial patience required pays off when you get fresh asparagus on your table to herald that spring has come, and of course it tastes a million times better than bought.

TO EAT

I steam or boil asparagus until it's tender and dip it in melted butter or the yolk of a soft-boiled egg. If you are eating asparagus alone, do it by moonlight – this crop demands a certain amount of reverence and ritual.

Drink

There's something deeply primal about creating liquid concoctions from
scratch: it brings out the temptress in me. The processes involved – picking,
crushing, distilling, brewing, fermenting – are all eerily seductive and
witchcrafty. I'm fascinated by flavour, and drinks, being less texturally
distracting than food, are a real eye-opener when it comes to incorporating
ingredients that we are perhaps more familiar with in terms of scent rather
than taste.

I love to put rosewater in herbal teas when I'm feeling virtuous, but these things
really come into their own when you have friends to entertain – and I tell you now that
little shots of wobbly rhubarb jelly laced with something alcoholic are never, ever dull.

So here are some ideas for plants to grow for drinking, along with some things to
hand round while you drink. Some require more commitment than others, but you
can always produce something delightful, even if it's just gin and tonic with ice and
a home-grown slice.

Rosewater

I'm tempted to say this is one for the girls, but whenever I make this, it gets everyone fascinated. The process is kind of geeky and scientific (which I love), but you also end up with the most delectable water, which can be used either for sprinkling on your pillow in those rare moments of relaxation, or as a toner if you're into that three-step skincare process. It's also a lovely thing to drop into herbal tea, and adds a delicate flavour to sponge cakes. It costs loads in the shops and nothing to make.

TIMING   Any time you have scented roses.

YOU WILL NEED   **A big bunch of roses** Cut off the stalks. You're supposed to use fresh, but I often do this with bought blooms that are just turning. The only stipulation is that they must be scented.
A brick
A big cooking pot with a domed lid I use a massive Le Creuset, but one of those French speckled stockpots would be even better.
A heatproof bowl One that will fit inside the pot when it's on top of the brick and the lid is put on upside down.
Some bags of ice cubes

METHOD   This is the process of distillation. Rip the petals off the roses, put the brick in the middle of the pot and place the petals around it so that they come to roughly just above the top of it. Then put the bowl on the brick and cover the roses with water, so that it's just submerging the bottom of the bowl. Put the lid on the pot upside down and bring the water to a rolling boil.

As soon as this happens, put the bags of ice on top of the upturned lid and turn the heat down so that you can hear the water simmering gently. The bowl will fill up with rosewater slowly as the water condenses on the cold lid. Lift the lid quickly and test the contents of the bowl periodically. It should smell and taste of roses, and you should have a good bowlful after about 40 minutes. Your kitchen will smell wonderful too.

Cool the distilled rosewater and bottle it. This makes a really special present if you can find one of those old French bottles, tie a ribbon round its neck and give it a brand-new cork.

AND MORE   I have always wanted to do this with orange flowers but can't get enough. It goes without saying that you can use this process with any flowers you love the smell of.

Rose geranium punch

This is a lovely drink for which I use the leaves of the rose-scented geranium called Pelargonium graveolens (commonly known as rose geranium), although as each scented-leaved pelargonium has its own distinct fragrance it would be well worth experimenting. I'm unable to resist buying little plugs of different varieties when I see them at flower shows, and I often flavour sponge cakes with the chopped leaves.

I make this punch in summer, either mixing it with something like sangria or leaving it to shine in its virgin state. If you want to go all out, make an ice punch bowl to serve it in.

THE LOWDOWN

Pelargoniums come mainly from South Africa and are frost-tender, so I grow them in pots in my kitchen and put them outside for the summer. They like full light, well-drained soil and good air circulation. I always keep them on the dry side, hardly watering them at all in winter and waiting until the compost is dry before I water at any other time.

Buy a rose-scented pelargonium and keep it in a pot filled with John Innes No. 2, feeding it in spring and early summer with a balanced liquid fertiliser every fortnight or so. Cut the plant back in early spring by about half to keep it nice and bushy.

TIMING

Summer.

FOR AN ICE BOWL
YOU WILL NEED

Pelargonium leaves and flowers
2 plastic mixing bowls One of which fits inside the other with a 5cm or so gap. Don't use glass bowls, as they sometimes crack when the water expands.
Duct tape
Sliced fruit Or use any other decorative stuff you have to hand.

FOR THE PUNCH
YOU WILL NEED

1 litre cloudy apple juice
200g caster sugar
6 *Pelargonium graveolens* leaves Or use other rose-scented pelargonium leaves.
Juice and zest of 4 limes

METHOD

First make the ice bowl. Get someone to help you hold the smaller bowl centred inside the larger one while you attach it at the rim with duct tape. When you've finished, it will be suspended, creating a bowl-shaped mould for water to flow into. Fill the bottom half of this mould with water, pelargonium leaves and flowers, and sliced fruit, and freeze the whole thing overnight; then repeat the process with the top half. Remove the ice bowl from its plastic prison by pouring some hot water into the central bowl and dipping the outer one in a sink full of hot water to loosen it.

To make the punch, simmer the apple juice, sugar and scented leaves until the sugar is dissolved (about five minutes); then add the lime juice and zest and leave to cool. Strain into your ice bowl or another receptacle.

Lemon verbena

This is one of those delectable plants that is visually unarresting but puts you into a trance with its scent. Of all the lemon-scented plants in the world, this is truly the most gorgeous.

THE LOWDOWN

Lemon verbena (*Aloysia triphylla*) is a deciduous perennial that comes originally from Chile and is therefore labelled half-hardy. This means that it won't deal with our winter and must be brought inside during the cold months, but I know of at least three proud owners in the south-east who have this planted outside in their sheltered gardens.

TIMING

Plant in spring.

YOU WILL NEED

1 *Aloysia triphylla* **plant** You can buy this plant in good nurseries and garden centres; you'll find it in the Herbs section.
Container 20cm diameter or larger.
Compost Use John Innes No. 2.
A handful of Osmacote granules (See page 229.)
A sheltered site Or a spot by a warm wall if you are planting outside, plus some grit and and bark chippings.

METHOD

If you're growing your lemon verbena in a container, a handful of slow-release fertiliser granules mixed into the compost will feed the pot for a year. In subsequent years you can either scrape off the top layer of compost and replace it with more compost and more granules, or feed it with a general liquid fertiliser every couple of weeks during the summer.

If you're trying your luck in the garden, put the plant near a warm wall and prepare the planting hole with some grit to provide drainage. It will also benefit from being mulched over in winter with something dry like bark chippings to keep its roots warm.

Make sure you keep it watered well during the growing season. It will flower in late summer – it has tiny lilac blooms – after which you can trim it to keep its shape. Move the plant inside before the first frosts in autumn and keep it on the dry side all winter.

You can harvest the leaves at any time during the growing season.

AND MORE

The leaves are even more pungent when dry, so bowls of these in your house will create a welcome stink. Lemon verbena tea is utterly delicious; just infuse the leaves in hot water, as you would with any tisane.

Rosehip syrup

My mother, being a war baby, used to dole out rosehip syrup as a general panacea when we were little. The sweetness of it made it a special treat — it was always administered neat on to a teaspoon from the bottle — and the ritual of it augmented its properties as a cure-all that healed anything from a grazed knee to sniffles, coughs and wheezes. I have a vague memory of being rather pleased at having contracted chicken pox because of the prospect of lashings of this sweet elixir. Now I use it, rather more seductively, as a cordial, or a sweetener for herbal teas, but nothing can quite compete with licking it off a teaspoon.

THE LOWDOWN
The best hips come from wild roses — *Rosa canina* or *R. rugosa*. The hips are what are left when the flowers have faded and dropped their petals. Wild roses will start to do this in late August, but it's best to go out and pick the hips in November, preferably after the first frosts. The hips are exceptionally rich in vitamin C, containing as much as sixty times the vitamin C of a comparable quantity of citrus fruit. Native Americans swore by it and therefore never had scurvy. The recipe below was the one given by the Ministry of Food during the Second World War.

TIMING
Autumn to winter.

YOU WILL NEED
About 800g rosehips You can find these growing in hedgerows and other people's gardens (or your own, if you are lucky).
A piece of muslin Or you can use a clean pair of tights.
About 600g granulated sugar Or more if you want.
Small sterile bottles or jars By this, I mean ones that have just come out of the dishwasher or have been washed in very hot water, using a bottle brush, and rinsed really well.

METHOD
Put the hips in a food processor and blitz them until they are properly nuked. Place them in a litre of boiling water and bring it back to the boil, remove from the heat and allow to stand for 15 minutes.

Strain this liquid through the muslin or tights, until the bulk of it has come through, and put what's left back in the pan with another litre of boiling water. Repeat the straining process with this second batch and put all the strained juice into a clean saucepan. Boil it down until you have about 1 litre of russet liquid. At this point add the sugar and boil for a further five minutes.

Pour the syrup into the bottles or jars and seal them, storing the precious tincture in a dark cupboard or the freezer. Once opened it has a shelf life (kept refrigerated) of about a week.

Wheatgrass

I'm not one of those people who get put off my takeaway whilst watching someone having liposuction on telly, and I can stomach weird food like pigs' trotters and creatures with tentacles, but the only thing I have ever tried which made me physically retch was a wheatgrass shot at one of those trendy juice bars. If you have a juicer and want to harvest it, be my guest, but I grow it because I think a bright green mini-lawn is rather modish and cool in a slightly kitsch way — and it's really easy to do as well.

THE LOWDOWN
Growing wheatgrass (*Triticum aestivum*) is just an extension of sprouting (see page 93), in which you're providing a solid base for the seeds and allowing them to develop leaves. Advocates of wheatgrass claim it can do extraordinary things, from simple detoxing to healing the terminally ill. There's no doubt that the bright, almost Day-Glo green of a tray of wheatgrass is essentially a cheering, happy thing to behold.

TIMING
You can do this at any time of year.

YOU WILL NEED
Organic wheat seeds Available at all good health food places.
Jam jar with muslin and elastic band
Seed tray with plastic lid
Compost I use John Innes No.1 or seed compost because it's finer than multi-purpose.

METHOD
Soak about five tablespoons of the seeds overnight and put them in the jam jar. Follow the recipe for Sprouting (see page 93), washing and rinsing twice a day until they are just beginning to sprout.

Fill your seed tray with compost, at least 3cm deep, dampen it by soaking the seed tray in water and cover the surface with the sprouted seeds. The seeds should be pretty tightly packed, but not on top of each other, so move any errant ones around with a pencil or dibber.

Cover the seeds with another layer of compost, no more than 1.5cm deep, and spray it with water to dampen. Cover the tray with its plastic lid and then put the whole thing by a window in the kitchen or somewhere warmish. I often grow wheatgrass in my propagator and it loves the temperature in there. After about three days the sprouts will be bursting into leaf, each one a triumphant spear of the finest, grassiest green. Remove them from the propagator or take the lid off the tray. You can start harvesting the leaves now, if you can bear to mutilate your lawn. Put the tray on the table for people to tickle their palms with — this stuff has major feel appeal.

AND MORE
I sometimes sow the sprouted seeds in tiny shot glasses filled with compost and serve them at supper as a kind of non *amuse-bouche*, which the brave can laboriously chew at with screwed-up faces in a valiant if misguided attempt to cancel out their alcohol consumption.

Borage for ice and fireworks

There is something about the true blueness of this edible flower that makes it more of a candidate for drinks than food. It is the easiest of plants to grow and contains large amounts of GLA (very good for you), but most importantly, it's the prettiest thing you can possibly do to a Pimm's — or any summer drink.

THE LOWDOWN *Borago officinalis* is a hardy annual. The delicacy of the butterfly-like flower is misleading, because this plant grows to about 60cm high with big, bristly leaves and square hollow stems. It comes originally from the Mediterranean but is naturalised in Northern Europe and America. It's very good for reducing a fever and is said to impart courage. You can grow it from seed anywhere you have a spare patch, and even in a large pot filled with multi-purpose compost. You need sow it only once, because it self-seeds everywhere. Or find a kind gardener who will let you pick theirs — highly likely, as most people have too much.

TIMING Borage flowers are out from early summer to mid-autumn, so this is the time to pick them. To sow your own, start in early spring.

TO GROW BORAGE YOU WILL NEED **A packet of borage seeds** Available from most garden centres.
A spare sunny spot
Well-drained soil (Like what they have in the Med.)

METHOD Sow the seeds by scattering them on weed-free crumbly soil (or compost if you are using a pot) and raking them in lightly. In due course pick the flowers and freeze them individually in ice cubes for your summer drinks.

AND MORE Here are a few other things you can do with borage:

❉ The leaves are deliciously cucumberish, so julienne them and put them into drinks, sandwiches, dips or cold soups.

❉ The incredibly pretty flowers can be used in pot-pourri or in little glasses to be gazed at.

❉ Jekka McVicar, queen of herbs, suggests a facial steam with borage leaves in boiling water, for those with dry skin.

❉ Much more exciting: toss a bouquet of borage on a fire, and the potash within will give you a mini fireworks display with little sparks and popping sounds.

Fiddleheads with bagna cauda

This is perhaps the poshest thing you can serve with drinks. You have to catch the fern just before it unfurls, and you absolutely must take care to get the right fern, or else you run the risk of making everyone ill. The taste is delicate, asparagussy, spinachy and light … but it's the shape of these little things that will really blow everyone away.

THE LOWDOWN

Edible fiddleheads come from a fern called *Matteucia struthiopteris* (the ostrich or shuttlecock fern). Ferns are muddling sometimes, so always ask for it by its Latin name to be sure. This deciduous fern comes from woodland in Europe, East Asia and North America, and it spreads by rhizomes (underground stems), which grow horizontally. If you have somewhere shady and damp, you could end up with a forest of these, which would be no bad thing. As long as the conditions are right, it will look after itself.

TIMING

Spring to summer.

YOU WILL NEED

***Matteucia struthiopteris* ferns** Available from garden centres.
A shady site with moist soil Or a large pot filled with a mixture of multi-purpose and John Innes No. 2 compost.

METHOD

Plant your ferns and give them a year or two to settle in and get big and strong before you start harvesting from them.

To harvest fiddleheads, watch carefully as the fronds appear in spring and then snap them off the plant at ground level before they've uncurled. Prepare them by washing really well, getting as much of the brown chaff off as possible – it's not harmful to eat, just unpretty.

Steam the fiddleheads over boiling water until they're al dente (some people say you can eat them raw, but it's safer to cook them) and serve to dip in bagna cauda (see below) or whatever you like. They're also very special steamed a little longer and coated in butter and lemon, or sautéed with lashings of butter.

TO MAKE BAGNA CAUDA

Melt **10 oily anchovies** with **5 cloves of crushed garlic** in **150ml very expensive olive oil**. Then whisk in **100g butter** until it's melted, removing the pan from the heat and whisking some more until the ingredients have amalgamated. Serve it hot with raw vegetables and fiddleheads.

Lemons for your drinks

There's something uniquely decadent about having your own lemons that I can't quite put my finger on, because it's not difficult to accomplish. You can buy standard lemon trees in pots at garden centres and although they're pricey, their evergreen prettiness makes them worth the cost. They'll tart up your home in winter and your terrace in summer, and produce deliciously scented flowers, not to mention lemons. The other good thing is that you don't need a conservatory, as citrus will adapt to low light levels: just put the whole thing outside in spring if you possibly can.

THE LOWDOWN   Lemons are evergreen trees and shrubs that come from open forest, thickets and scrub in South East Asia and the Pacific Islands. They are frost-tender, which means that anything below 3°C is pushing it, especially if you want fruit, so wait until the temperature outside is about equal to indoors before you move them outside, keeping a careful watch out for late spring frosts, which will kill the new shoots. They like ericaceous (acidic) compost that is well drained, and, if at all possible, only rainwater.

TIMING   It's best to re-pot your tree in spring.

YOU WILL NEED   **A tree** Make sure it's a lemon (*Citrus limon*), unless you want clementines (*C. reticulata*) or oranges (*C. aurantium or C. sinensis*). If you want all these, that's easy too, because they all like the same treatment. For lemons, look for a variety called 'Meyer', which is dwarf, growing up to a very manageable 2m, and therefore perfect for a pot. They're available online and sold as standards in many a posh nursery.
A terracotta container Slightly larger than the container it's already in. Terracotta is best because these plants simply hate to be wet, and plastic tends to hold in moisture.
Loam-based, ericaceous compost Available in bags. Mix it with grit if you can only get loam-free.
Pot feet and tray If you are growing your lemon indoors.
Water-soluble feed such as Miraclegro

METHOD   The first thing to do with your tree is re-pot it in your container. Don't bury the roots too deep in the compost, as they like being near the surface.
　　With watering, the trick is to avoid extremes. As long as the drainage is good, and you never allow the pot to stand in water, it's easy to keep lemons happy by soaking them twice a week in the growing season, until you can see the water coming out of the bottom of the pot. Indoors, this will mean that you'll need to have a tray underneath to prevent the floor getting wet, so buy some pot feet to raise the pot off the saucer, to ensure it is clear of the standing water.
　　Between spring and autumn, feed with a water-soluble feed such as Miraclegro, diluted in a watering can according to the instructions on the

packet. This will keep nutrient levels high so that the plant can flower and fruit. Do this every time you water, or at least once a week.

In winter, keep the plant barely moist and don't feed it – there's no point, as it's not growing. Keep the plant as far as possible from the central heating; an unheated room is best. If this is not possible, at least keep the humidity up by grouping it with other plants and standing it above a tray of water either on pot feet or stones.

It's nice to move the plant outdoors in summer, and here again, avoid extremes, so gradually acclimatise the plant to higher light levels – by putting it under a tree or in a doorway so that it's shaded for a couple of weeks – before it goes out in the sun.

To set fruit, the flowers need pollinating, and if the plant stays indoors all year, you may need to help it by brushing the pollen from one flower to another, using a make-up brush or just by shaking the whole thing gently. Outside, insects will do this for you.

AND MORE Little standard lemon trees in pots are glorious anywhere, but if you have more than one, they seem to cry out to be lined up. Just a thought … And always, always drink your gin and tonic sitting next to the tree that gave you that lovely slice.

Rhubarb for vodka jelly

*I really, really love rhubarb, for its eating potential as well as its ornamental value.
If you have a spare patch of ground anywhere, or even a large container of about 50cm
in diameter (fill it with John Innes No. 2), rhubarb should be in it.*

THE LOWDOWN
Rhubarb (*Rheum*) is a hardy perennial that comes from Siberia – which is
extremely good news for a virgin, because it means that it will thrive in the
harshest of conditions. That's why it's so often found in neglected gardens,
doing very nicely thank you. You buy it in one-year-old crowns (as you do
asparagus), and as with all these things, there are numerous varieties to
choose from. I have no idea which mine is, but I am told that 'Cawood
Delight' and 'Victoria' are very good.

TIMING
Plant in winter and harvest in summer.

YOU WILL NEED
Rhubarb crowns Available from large garden centres and specialist
suppliers (see page 262).
Organic farmyard manure or garden compost
General fertiliser such as Growmore

Plant the crowns in December, burying them 2.5cm below the soil, and water
them in if the ground is very dry. Give them a mulch of organic farmyard
manure or garden compost, making sure that you place this in a circle around
where the stem will emerge. This is a big, lush plant, so give each one half a
metre or more to grow in.

Things will start to happen after about a month and you should apply some
general fertiliser such as Growmore in February. You can stop right there if
all you are after is lush, tropical-looking foliage, but if you want to harvest,
do the following.

Make sure that you cut off the flowerheads as soon as they appear in
early spring. By doing this you will make the rhubarb think that something
disastrous has happened and it will concentrate on making itself bigger and
stronger rather than making seed. You can harvest from May to July, as soon
as the leaves are open, but it is best to wait until the second year to pick your
first crop, and even then, only pick a couple of stems per plant.

You pick a stem by getting your hand as far down the stem as possible
and twisting as you pull. After the second year you can pull the largest stalks
with abandon, but always leave two or three per plant. The result is utterly
delicious, but may need peeling. And please don't ever eat the leaves – they
are poisonous.

AND MORE
If you want sweeter, more tender stems, you need to force them. This
couldn't be easier, although you lose the plant's ornamental value because you
have to exclude light as soon as you see the plant emerge from the ground.

You do this with a rhubarb forcer (a bell-shaped terracotta urn, available new or at reclamation yards); or you could use something like an up-ended dustbin, but they're not very pretty. This will make the plant think it is still underground and grow as fast as possible to find the light. You get an early crop this way (within four weeks). When you've picked your crop, remove the cover and leave the plant until next year.

TO DRINK

A few stems of rhubarb can produce enough jewel-like liquor to make a bowl of jelly, with pulp left over to spoon greedily into your own mouth. Cut **some rhubarb stems** into chunks and put them in an ovenproof glass dish with **½ litre of water** and **3 or 4 handfuls of granulated sugar** (or to taste). Cover and cook for an hour or so in the oven at 190°C/gas mark 5. Strain this, add quite a bit of vodka and make jelly, following the instructions on your packet of gelatine.

Pickled onions for proper cocktails

I have an abiding memory (or was it a fantasy?) from childhood of being taken to a cocktail party whilst on a summer holiday in North Wales. There were ladies in neon swirling maxi-dresses, with cigarette holders and up-dos. There was a bar with stools, and a brown shagpile carpet, there was Cinzano and cheese and pineapple, and there were delicious pickled onions on cocktail sticks. In other words, it was a proper cocktail party — no messing about. My parents were far too boring ever to hold such a glorious event and I have naturally resented them ever since. It's time for a revival.

THE LOWDOWN Mini onions are simply man-selected cultivars of normal bulb onions (*Allium cepa*), grown close together so that they stay small.

TIMING Start in mid- to late spring.

YOU WILL NEED **Onion seed** You can get onion cultivars perfect for pickling, such as 'Paris Silverskin' or the pinky-hued 'Purplette'.
A pot or trough at least 15cm deep filled with John Innes No. 3 Or a weed-free sunny patch which is well drained (add some grit) and has been forked over a few weeks before planting with some nice nutritious garden compost.

METHOD In a pot, scatter the seeds thinly and cover them with about 1.5cm of compost. In the ground, sow a little patch of short rows that you've made with your finger and cover them over. Water them carefully with a watering can that has a rose, so that you don't displace any of the seeds, and wait for them to appear. When this happens, thin them out by gently pulling out seedlings so that the ones that are left are about 2–3cm apart. This spacing will give you dinky little onions the size of the end of your thumb. Let them grow for about ten weeks, keeping them watered and watching for weeds, and then pull them out and shake the dirt off them.

TO PICKLE For pickled onions, you need to dry them first. It's best to do this outdoors (obviously out of the rain) for about a week to ten days. Then cut off the leaves and any roots and peel them carefully so that they're all shiny and clean, making use of any nearby children or friends.
　　Check them over for the slightest sign of softness or rot and throw any suspect ones away before soaking the rest for 24 hours in cold brine made from boiling **1 litre water** with **500g salt**. Make sure they're submerged by weighing them down with something. Rinse them well, pack them into a pickling jar, pour over **good-quality malt vinegar** – the kind that induces a gush of saliva with one pungent whiff – and leave them for as long as you like, but at least a week. Serve on the end of a toothpick with good old-fashioned cocktails and possibly a game of bridge.
　　And of course they're fabulous in salads.

Sweet violets

My love affair with violets began relatively recently when I was visiting a garden in November and I saw a violet in flower at the front of a border. As it was November there wasn't too much else to distract me, and I got down on my knees to sniff. The scent was out of this world: sweetly floral without being cloying, with a sultry, earthy note (or was that because my nose was almost touching the soil?)

There's something so all-encompassing about violets. They were the favoured bloom of Empresses Josephine and Eugénie and a symbol of the House of Bonaparte; the starting point of so many of the world's most sophisticated and luxurious perfumes; beloved of Queen Victoria; and sold in their millions at London and Paris markets by all the Eliza Doolittles – luverly. Now violet flavouring is experiencing something of a retro revival, enhancing creams encased in chocolate and designer muffins. So here are some of my favourites for culinary adventures, or simply olfactory gratification.

THE LOWDOWN
The violets sold as bedding plants at most garden centres are commonly known as pansies. These are cultivars created from lots of complicated cross-breeding. They come in a multitude of colours and are brilliant for brightening up any space, and eating in salads, but not for scent. For this recipe it's important to buy scented violets from specialist nurseries or violet farms (see page 262). These bloom in late winter and early spring with blue or white flowers, and originate from temperate regions like ours. They'll be happy either in pots or in the ground, in full sun or partial shade, as long as the soil is fertile and well drained.

TIMING
Winter.

MY FAVOURITE VIOLAS
***Viola odorata* (English violet or sweet violet)** Comes in many forms. I like one called 'Devon Violet' – often found growing wild in Devon – and a white one called 'Alba'.
V. **'The Czar'** Deep purple with a white eye.
V. **'Baronne Alice de Rothschild'** Large and dark.
V. **'Conte di Brazza' and** *V.* **'Hopley's White'** These are Parma violets, so they are slightly more tender and will need to be kept frost-free in winter (for frost protection, see page 235), but they are worth the effort for their heavy perfume and double flowers (yum).

VIOLET CHAMPAGNE
My collection of violets is too small and precious to produce flowers in the quantities needed for syrup, but I get around this by buying myself a present every year (around Valentine's Day, actually) of a posy of sweet violets. When they are about to go over I make a syrup.

YOU WILL NEED
15–20 violet blooms Remove the stalks.
150ml water
Granulated sugar

METHOD   Bring the water to a boil and add the flowers, stirring them together well, and remove from the heat. Let them infuse for 24 hours. Weigh the liquid, return it to the heat and add double that weight of sugar, stirring it into the liquid until it eventually dissolves. Leave the whole thing for three days, stirring it whenever you remember, and then heat it gently until it reaches the consistency of a pouring syrup. I serve this with champagne (when I'm feeling generous) – a small drop at the bottom of a glass will make a sort of violet Kir royale which is delicious, and especially pretty with the flowers suspended in the syrup. I also lick it off the spoon or use it to sweeten herbal tea.

AND MORE   If you love doing fiddly stuff, it's very easy to make crystallised petals, which you can decorate cakes with. Using a small paintbrush, cover individual petals with whisked egg white, shower them with granulated sugar and allow to dry. Yes, you probably do have better things to do … in which case, it's a very good way of keeping children safely occupied for an hour or two.

Elderflower bubbly

This is summer in a glass: lazy, hazy and only mildly intoxicating. It's a doddle to make, and if you're a virgin to foraging, it's an excellent way to start.

THE LOWDOWN The elder (*Sambucus nigra*) is a deciduous shrub which sometimes thinks it's a tree. It will grow almost anywhere: it's one of those pioneer plants that takes hold and grows really fast – a good virgin-pleaser. It's a great thing to have in your garden if you have the space for it (it can grow up to 6m tall and wide if you don't keep it under control). It comes from woodland thickets in Europe, North Africa and South West Asia. The elder has been cultivated by man for centuries and used medicinally and as a dye. Most importantly, though, its stems, which can be hollowed out, have provided generations of children with pea-shooters.

If you don't have the space for an elder, it's easy to find one. Look for its toothed leaves, light brown, thick, ridged bark and umbels of creamy-white flowers that smell sweeeeeeet. Don't be put off by the alarmingly musky, cat's-pee-like undertone – that's the leaves.

Actually, it's worth getting a little geek's handbook to trees and shrubs which will help to identify these things – I have a *Reader's Digest Field Guide* which I carry everywhere with me (though no cagoule or walking boots, I'm afraid). It really is important to check that what you're picking is the right thing. The best time to do that is before you pick it, so that you can use all the characteristics of the plant to identify it (elderflower umbels are very similar to cow-parsley flowers, which you certainly wouldn't want to eat – but these don't grow on shrubs or trees).

TIMING Elderflowers are out and at their best in June and July.

YOU WILL NEED **8 large elderflower heads**
1¼kg granulated sugar
8 litres water
2 lemons (unwaxed)
4 tablespoons mild white wine vinegar
A piece of muslin
Bottles Glass bottles with screw caps are best because they don't let so much fizz out, but plastic will do. Make sure they're really clean, and that means using them straight from the dishwasher or washing them in very hot water, using a bottle brush, and rinsing them well.

METHOD   Get a big pot and heat the sugar and water in it until the sugar is dissolved. Leave this to cool completely. Then add the washed elderflower heads, the rind of the lemons (removed with a potato peeler) and their juice, and the vinegar. Cover the pot and leave it for 24 hours.

Strain the whole lot through the muslin into bottles, squeezing the flowers in the muslin until you get the last drop out. (It's a good idea to place each bottle inside a bowl in case the liquid overflows.)

Store the bottles in a cool place like a cellar or garage (not having either of these, I use a cupboard in an unheated room). It will be ready (i.e. fermented and bubbly) in about a fortnight. Serve it cold, to people you adore.

This will keep for up to two years and the taste will improve as it matures. Once opened, as long as you have screw-cap bottles, it will stay fizzy and delicious for weeks on end in the fridge.

My favourite thing is to serve this at Christmas, to remind people that spring will come again.

Grow

I guess all of us have had the experience of being led to excess by fabulous pictures in colour supplements, and the world of plants is no different from anything else in this respect. Fashion is key in gardening, in that it inspires and attracts us to plants we may not have known about or tried to grow before. But watching a seed germinate and grow that you have planted yourself is so utterly miraculous that the picture on the packet that inspired you in the first place often pales into insignificance – I promise you, I am undone, every time it happens.

These projects are all about learning new stuff: from discovering the secret to making a good compost and taking a more detailed look at how plants reproduce, to information on how to nurture plants like orchids and carnivorous plants that need specific treatment to flourish.

Go forth and grow.

Sweet peas – sowing seed

A few years ago I sowed the contents of a packet of sweet peas that my mother had given me some time before. The extent of my knowledge about plants was that they looked nice, and that was it. I followed the instructions on the packet. They grew. Now I am writing this book. If you sow some seeds, you will find out how easy it is to surround yourself with masses of gorgeous plants; and by default you'll be furnished with a deeper understanding of how this stuff works. For me, that opened doors I didn't know existed.

THE LOWDOWN
Sweet peas (*Lathyrus odoratus*) are hardy annual climbers. This means that they grow, set seed and die all in one year and can be grown outdoors. They are perfect seeds for a virgin because they're big enough to handle (unlike some other seeds, which are almost dust-like), and also because the payoff is huge: they'll give you loads of little vases of scented flowers all summer long.

TIMING
I sow sweet peas in March and April, but you can sow them in the autumn to get much earlier flowers, if you have the space and time to spare (I don't). Additionally, you can sow right up to the end of May, which would also extend your sweet pea season, if you are very organised (I am not).

YOU WILL NEED
Sweet pea seeds *Lathyrus odoratus* 'Matucana' has the strongest scent, but there are hundreds of different varieties to choose from. I often buy mixed packets for the surprise factor.
Compost You can either get a bag of special seed compost, or use ordinary multi-purpose compost if you like. The important thing to remember is that, just as you wouldn't feed a baby with red wine and foie gras, seeds do not want nutrient-rich compost, as it would make them ill.
Horticultural grit
A modulated seed tray or some root trainers These come with a plastic lid. You can use any type of pot or container, though, as long as you make sure it's completely clean and has drainage holes, and use a plastic bag and an elastic band instead of a lid.
A container See overleaf.
Something for the sweet peas to scramble up See overleaf.

METHOD
Put some lukewarm water in a glass and put the seeds in, and then leave them overnight. If you have a radiator, put the glass on that to keep the water warmish. Not all seeds need soaking – it'll tell you on the back of the packet if you need to.

Mix your compost half and half with the grit so that you end up with something that feels light and comfy, and then fill your tray or pot with it, and tap it down gently. Then water the whole thing, either by placing the pot or tray in another tray of water and waiting until the top of the soil is glistening, or by soaking from above with the fine rose of a watering can. You can try to

water from above without a rose, but the compost will be displaced and it will be messy.

When your compost is damp you can place the seeds in it. The back of the packet will tell you how deep they want to be, but the general rule is to put the seed under the soil at twice its own depth. With very fine seed, this means scattering it on the surface, but with sweet peas it means about 3mm deep.

Put the top on the tray, or fashion some other kind of top with a piece of glass, or even a clear plastic sandwich bag tied around your pot with an elastic band. The important thing here is to provide warmth and humidity. For most seeds, light is not a requirement until later. Now label your seeds with a name and a date, because you will forget. Put the whole thing somewhere out of the way and check on it each day for signs of germination.

As soon as you see little green shoots, the lid comes off. The object here is to treat these seedlings as meanly as they can bear. This means that the temperature must go down and the air circulation must go up, and at this stage you need to give them light – a windowsill is perfect, as long as no frost is forecast. If you keep them too warm and snug they'll grow lank and drippy.

In a few weeks, the plants will develop their first true leaves – different in size and shape from the first seed leaves. When the little plants have two pairs of true leaves it's a good idea to pinch off the leading shoot (i.e. the one pointing towards the sky). This will make the plants bushier as all their energy will go into the remaining sideshoots, and that means more flowers for your beautiful home.

By this time the seedlings will be ready to go to their permanent home. Remove them from the seed trays, being careful not to handle them by their stems. Pick them up gently by holding on to one of the leaves instead, and ease them out of their nursery bed by using something long and pointed, so that you disturb the roots as little as possible. This is where modulated seed trays or root trainers come into their own, as all you need to do to get seedlings out is gently prod the underside of the plastic, or open up the root trainers.

PLANTING OUT To plant them in their new home, you just make a hole in the new compost or soil that's big enough to contain the roots, gently ease the plant in and firm it in, making sure the roots are all covered and the plant is nicely tucked in to its new bed. Then water the whole thing until you can see water running out of the bottom of the container; or, if you're transplanting the seedlings into a flowerbed, water so that the area around them has been properly soaked. Because it is a climber, a sweet pea plant needs something to scramble up. For this you can use any suitable climbing frame. The plant climbs by using tendrils, which are basically modified leaves that have learned to spiral around things, pulling the plant upwards as they go, so as to get it off the ground and towards the light, which it needs in order to make food. In the wild, this would mean it using other plants for support, and you could indeed plant your seedlings near a shrub and let them go for it – very pretty. But because you want to have lots of gorgeous-smelling flowers, and because you may indeed not even have a garden, let alone any shrubs that might lend themselves to this task, it's going to be easier to get at them if the support is of your own making. Here are some ways to grow them:

❋ Get a large container. An old wooden box lined with plastic lends itself very well to this, but any deep container will do, like a window box, or just a normal terracotta pot. Make sure it is at least 20cm deep (because *Lathyrus* like a nice deep root run) and fill it with compost. If you're using an old wooden box which you have to line, make sure that you've made holes in the plastic at the bottom of the box so that water can run out of the slats. This time you can use ordinary multi-purpose compost without grit, or a loam-based compost, such as John Innes No. 2, or a mixture of both.

Stick some long, twiggy sticks, at least 1.5m high, into the compost. Willow or hazel sticks are very good for this purpose; you can buy them from florists or go out and find your own. Place these sticks either in a line or an oval or a circle, depending on the proportions of the container. What you want to end up with is a twiggy dome or wall that the plants will scramble up and form a wonderful living scented mound or screen. Plant one or two healthy seedlings either side of the base of each twig.

❋ Put up some netting (this is particularly wonderful on a balcony) and plant your seedlings in deep long containers at the base of it so that the plants can climb up and you'll have a glorious wall of scented sweet peas enclosing your space.

❋ If all I have is just one pot, I use a wigwam of bamboo canes pushed into the soil at equal intervals and tied together at the top. Because bamboo is slippery it's a good idea to wrap string around the whole lot in a circle so as to provide some horizontal support for the tendrils to cling to; or you could cover the entire framework with some kind of netting.

With all support systems, you will initially have to tie the stems in (gently) with garden twine to get them started in the right direction.

PICKING THE FLOWERS   Your sweet peas should start flowering in June and keep going all summer long if you keep them sweet by watering them. The utterly glorious thing about this plant is that you have to pick it – if you don't, it won't produce more flowers because all its energy will go into setting seed. So as soon as it starts blooming, start picking. Cut the flowers at the base of their stem and put them in little vases – I like them in those cheap Moroccan tea glasses; or use the milk jug from your granny's china tea set – anything small and pretty will do. Put them with other little annuals if you like (cornflowers are lovely with them), but they are just perfect on their own.

Spring bulbs in baskets

There is something so immediate and new-lifeish about a little basket filled with bulbs that they work very well for those myriad baby-worship outings that are compulsory when friends start breeding.

THE LOWDOWN | A bulb is a storage organ containing all the food the plant needs to grow. Spring bulbs grow, produce seed and use their leaves to do that old thing of converting light into sugar using their leaves, which feeds the bulb for next year. Unless you're planting really big baskets, it's best to use small bulbs for this, as most baskets are too shallow to support tall plants.

TIMING | It's nice to do this a few weeks before you give them away, so that the green spikes are making their way through the moss. Spring bulbs are available from mid-summer time, so if you're really organised you can do your planting well, well in advance.

YOU WILL NEED | **Spring bulbs** You can get these in mixed or separated packets from every nursery or garden centre. Look for crocuses, muscari, dwarf irises, dwarf tulips and dwarf daffodils. I prefer one type per basket, but there are no rules.
Lined baskets You can get these at florists and flower markets, with or without handles in a variety of different shapes and sizes. You can line a basket yourself with a cut-up bin liner. Lay it inside the basket, tuck in the edges and either staple or sew it in.
Multi-purpose compost
Sphagnum moss
Ribbon Preferably proper silk.

METHOD | Make sure the plastic lining of each basket has some holes in it. If not, cut some yourself by pinching the plastic and snipping with scissors – the holes need to be about the size that a hole-puncher would make, or larger, so that water can find its way out.

Fill the baskets with a layer of compost and cram the bulbs in, pointed end up, so that they're almost touching. The amount of soil on top should be the same depth as the bulbs. Cover the surface with moss and water the whole thing in the sink until you can see water running out of the bottom of the basket. Leave the baskets somewhere out of the way, keeping the soil damp but not sodden, until the bulb spikes emerge, and then tie a silk ribbon round the handle and see if you can bear to give it away.

AND MORE | If it's Easter, place little chocolate eggs on the moss and tie a yellow ribbon round the basket.

A big basket filled with little spring bulbs on the centre of a table is also a beautiful thing and lasts for ages, so long as you keep the bulbs watered and give them a spell outside at night-time.

157

Pelargoniums – taking cuttings

Pelargoniums are a joy. My absolute favourites are the scented-leaved varieties, of which I buy more and more every year. You can get them anywhere, but it's best to go to one of the many flower shows around the country where there will almost certainly be a stand full of them to choose from. It's like buying sweets that don't make you fat. I have them in little pots in my kitchen all year round. When you touch the leaves, you release the scent, which can be reminiscent of anything from warm spicy cinnamon to sharp, vibrant citrus.

THE LOWDOWN   Pelargoniums, often referred to as geraniums, are a massive genus of half-hardy or frost-tender shrubs first collected in South Africa. (For winter frost protection, see page 235.) Most like a sunny place, and can be grown in pots, hanging baskets, window boxes and in the open ground. If they like you, they'll flower continuously from spring to late autumn. Pelargoniums are ideal for taking cuttings from. This is vegetative propagation – all the offspring will be genetically identical to the parent. It couldn't be easier.

TIMING   You can take pelargonium cuttings at any time of year, but the best time is between spring and autumn (May to August is perfect). Otherwise you'll need to start messing around with providing bottom heat.

YOU WILL NEED   **A pelargonium plant**
Cuttings compost Cuttings need a rooting medium that is supportive, sterile, water retentive and well aerated. There are lots of different possibilities (special gels, vermiculite, etc.), but I use 50 per cent bought seed and cutting compost mixed with 50 per cent horticultural grit.
A clean container I use a small plastic pot that has been run through the dishwasher.
Dibber This is a fancy word for anything you choose to use to make a hole in the compost for your cutting. I use a pencil, nail or knitting needle. For obvious reasons it's good if you can find something that's a little bigger than the size of the cutting.
Larger pots for potting up See below.

METHOD   Prepare your container by filling it with the compost and grit mixture and tap it to settle the contents, and then label it. Take your plant and find some non-blooming sideshoots that are about 10cm long from base to tip. Pull one off gently with a downward motion so that you end up with a little strip of tissue on the end. This is called a heel. Carefully remove the leaves above this by snapping them cleanly over your thumbnail so that you are left with a naked stem and two or three leaves at the top.

   Now with your dibber make a hole as deep as the length of the stem you have below the first leaf. Put your cutting in the hole, making sure there is contact between the end of the cutting and the compost at the bottom of the hole, and then firm the compost gently around it. Cuttings like company when they're rooting, so repeat this with as many cuttings as will fill the pot without the leaves touching each other. Tap the container when you've finished to settle it.

Now soak the whole thing either by watering through the fine rose of a watering can or by putting the pot in a tray of water until the surface is glistening, and cover the surface with some more grit.

Put the whole thing somewhere light like a windowsill and wait, checking periodically to make sure the compost doesn't dry out. In a few weeks the leaves will start growing, and that means that the cutting has taken root and you have a new plant. I pot cuttings up individually in loam-based potting compost (John Innes No. 1 or 2) when I see the roots coming out of the holes at the bottom of the container.

AND MORE   If you like taking cuttings, you can get involved and start using exciting things like hormone rooting powder, and surgeon's blades, and propagators, and grow lights (see Good reading, page 263) – this is just the start of a whole new realm of geekdom. Enjoy.

Expanding the emerald bank — division

When I first became aware of the concept of dividing a plant up at the roots in order to make it grow more prolifically I was appalled. I imagined how I would feel if I were hauled out of bed, ripped unceremoniously down the middle, each half of me put into separate beds, doused with water and told to get on with it … But that was before I found out (to my great relief) that many plants thrive on this kind of treatment.

Dividing plants is a little unnerving at first, and that is why it's best to start off with Soleirolia soleirolii, because it's so forgiving in this respect (even a tiny piece will take root). I use this plant everywhere, inside and out. I love it for its beauty, its gorgeous fresh greenhousey smell and its soft, spongy, pillow-like texture, and its trailing, creeping habit, which means that it will cover the surface of a pot of compost in no time and then start spilling over the sides. Most of all I love it because I can rip bits off it and stick them anywhere, and they will get on with the business of growing. The common name for this plant is 'mind your own business'.

THE LOWDOWN | 'Mind your own business', or 'mother of thousands', or 'baby's tears', is a vigorous evergreen perennial that comes from shady places in the Mediterranean. It is fully hardy in the UK, although if it's hit by a bad frost it'll sulk for a while but will come right back in the spring. This plant is perfect for softening the cracks between paving or steps – in fact it's so good at growing that if it likes your space you may have to be quite careful about keeping it under control. For this reason, I grow it mainly in pots. It likes things shady and moist, and comes in three colours: golden-green, variegated silver and bog-standard normal (gorgeous) green.

TIMING | If you're using this plant outside, spring is the best time for this project, but you can do it pretty much any time of the year if you keep your pots indoors, as long as they are near a window.

YOU WILL NEED | **1 small pot of *Soleirolia soleirolii*** Sometimes sold under the name of *Helxine*, this is available in most garden centres. Better still, you can ask someone to give you a piece of theirs and divide that.
A pot filled with loam-based potting compost John Innes No. 1 works well. If you're planting outside, any normal garden soil will do, as long as it's fine – this plant won't perform properly if there are lots of big 'bits' in the soil. If you're using the cracks between paving stones, you should brush in some potting compost to give the plant a good start.

METHOD | Take the plant out of its pot and remove any excess soil. Then literally rip it with your hands or cut it with a knife into as many sections as you want, making sure each piece has some roots attached.

If you're using a pot, any shape will do, and it's really vital – because this plant is so low growing – that you build the compost into a mound, proud of the top of the pot (it will anyway sink a little). Put a section of plant into the middle of the pot, making sure the roots are roughly buried, and then water it. It will look rather lonely and ridiculous – a little tuft in the middle of a sea of brown – but before long the plant will start to expand outwards and, depending on the time of year and light levels, it will cover a large area in a gratifyingly short space of time.

It's always better to water this from below, using a saucer as a reservoir underneath your pot, so that you don't flatten the foliage.

AND MORE   Teeny little terracotta pots of this make great presents, especially if you nestle something fabulous in the middle (a diamond ring, for example).

Leafmould

Despite not having a garden, I still make leafmould, primarily because it does my tiny space so much good in the form of a mulch, and secondly because it makes me feel virtuous (the ultimate state of being for a virgin). Oh, and it requires practically zero effort.

THE LOWDOWN   Leafmould is made from fallen leaves that are allowed to rot down and decompose over a long time, creating a crumbly dark organic material, which can be used in lots of ways. It is a component of all soil (it usually gets there when leaves drop to the ground and are not cleared away but allowed to break down naturally). It is different from garden compost as we know it (see page 172) in that the decomposition process is aided by fungi rather than bacteria, and because of this it takes longer to make; but unlike compost, it doesn't need any attention in the form of temperature control or turning.

If you put leafmould around your plants, it will improve their lives immeasurably, improving the soil and helping to keep moisture in, and so reducing the need to water. You can use it in this way as a mulch, or you can work it into garden compost (see page 172) to make it lighter and generally better and more wholesome. You can also make your own potting compost out of it. You can never have enough of it, so make as much as you have room for, and use it all year round.

TIMING   Autumn.

YOU WILL NEED   **Leaves** Collect these from your garden or local park (ask first) in the autumn when they fall. Try not to use evergreen leaves (conifer needles or holly, etc.), and if you're collecting leaves from the street, make sure they're not contaminated by other rubbish or dog poo.
Black bin liners

METHOD   Simply scoop up the leaves and put them in the plastic bags, spray them with a little water and pack them tightly, tying up the bag at the neck. Punch a few holes in the bags with a garden fork and put them somewhere out of sight (I use the space under the steps leading to my front door). Leave them for eighteen months to two years. The result is a glorious material that can be used as described above.

Keep making leafmould every year and you will have a continuous supply. Some people like to shred their leaves first, or chop them up with a lawn-mower. This does aid the decomposition process somewhat, which means they get the finished product slightly sooner, but, not owning any such special equipment, I make use of my forgetful nature instead, which seems to speed up the whole process wonderfully.

AND MORE As you're doing this in the autumn, you might wish to get slightly Blue-Peter-ish and use some of the leaves you've collected to make wrapping paper for Christmas. Pick out leaves you particularly like. Any will do, but if you want your wrapping to look all modish and professional, stick to one type. Lay them out on some cheap paper (and here you can use literally anything you like, including old newspaper) and secure each leaf in place with the merest splodge of Pritt Stick so that it doesn't move about during spraying. Spray with any colour in the spectrum (gold is always good) or, for a nostalgic home-made effect, get children to paint over the leaves. When everything is dry, remove the leaves and do the same again on more paper, this time laying the leaves down unpainted side up, so that you cover the other side of them. You can then use them to decorate your presents, or your table.

Indoor blossom – forcing

My granny used to make indoor flower arrangements using blossom in wide shallow bowls, held down by a multitude of stones and clips and what have you. Looking close up at the blossom opening forms one of my earliest 'plant' memories. My granny didn't have a garden, so she must have bought her blooms at vast expense from a florist – a form of madness repeated by me over and over again in my twenties, when I used to decorate my flat for parties with the precious twigs.

Cut branches of blossom are rightly expensive: they're delicate and difficult to transport, and it takes time and commitment to grow trees and shrubs. The interesting thing is the number of people who actually own something which can give them early spring colour and scent indoors but do not use it. There are so many branches that are suitable for this kind of effect. Look in your own garden; or look in your neighbour's, and start being nice to them right away. A branch of blossom is utterly failsafe when it comes to decorating with flowers: it is always beautiful, whatever blossom you use and whatever the receptacle for it. It really is impossible to screw this up.

MY FAVOURITE SPRING BEAUTIES

Amelanchier Fabulously fragrant white blossom, easy to force.
Cherry and plum (*Prunus*) White and pink and deliciously scented.
Cornelian cherry (*Cornus mas*) Amazing yellow blossom. Good substitute for witch hazel if you have limey soil.
Crab apple (*Malus*) White or pink blossom with yummy scent.
Forsythia Yellow and very easy to force.
Honeysuckle (*Lonicera*) Make sure it's a scented one.
Magnolia Exquisite, but don't try to force it: just cut it as it's coming out.
Pear (*Pyrus*) White and smells wonderful.
Pussy willow (*Salix caprea/Salix discolor*) Beautiful, velvety, sexy.
Witch hazel (*Hamamelis*) Spooky fire-cracker blossom, very early January, and scented too.

THE LOWDOWN

While it's lovely to have blossom before it would normally come out, just bringing in a branch full of blossom to appreciate close up is an equal pleasure and a lot less hassle. The suggestions below will provide the optimum conditions for long-lasting, beautiful blossoming branches indoors, and are worth following, particularly if you have spent money on them. There are also suggestions, though, for how to cut and force your blossom to open early. There is only one rule here: spring = cool, bright and wet. These are the conditions you want to replicate for best results.

TIMING

Blossom appears in the spring.

Branches of unopened blossom For suitable shrubs, see opposite.
Secateurs or a sharp knife
Hammer
A cool, dark place

METHOD   If you buy branches, choose those with the least number of open buds, get
them home as quickly as possible and, using secateurs or a sharp knife, re-cut
the stems at an angle. Bash the ends with a hammer to crush them and put the
twigs in water. It's very important that the branches do not dry out too fast.
You want to mimic the cool moist feeling of spring as far as possible, so the
blossom will last longer if it's kept in an unheated room for the majority of
the time, and would love it if you sprayed it with a fine mist of water every
now and then. But I fully understand that life may be rather too short for all
that, in which case just make sure you keep the water fresh.

If you are cutting your own, follow the above instructions if the blossom is
starting to show. Otherwise, you can force the blossom by doing the following.

Choose some branches with blossom buds that are tightly closed. You're
likely to find these when it's cold outside – too cold for insects to venture out
and pollinate anything – and therefore it would be awfully wasteful for the
plant to be in flower. Cut the branches with a sharp knife or secateurs, making
sure they're long enough for whatever purpose you have in mind. I usually cut
one branch that has smaller branches or twigs coming off it, rather than lots
of little ones. This will often take up a space of a cubic metre or more, so if
you want something big and majestic like that, make sure you have enough
space. Otherwise small twigs of about 30–50cm look lovely.

As soon as you get them inside, submerge the entire branch in lukewarm
water for 24 hours to trick them into thinking that spring has come. With
large branches this will be difficult, so mist the branch three or four times
instead. All this should happen in an unheated room like a cellar. Then smash
the ends of the twigs or branches and put them in water in an unheated room
with as much light as possible, like a conservatory, making sure they don't dry
out and misting them every day when you remember. Some branches take
longer than others to force, but you can expect to see some blossom action in
anything between one and six weeks, depending on what you're forcing.

The above will give the optimum forcing results, but I often cut branches
and bring them straight into a heated room, misting them when I remember.
This process is less gentle – too hot and too dark – and I get a shorter bloom
time as a result, but I don't have a conservatory, so there.

Moth orchid nurture

Moth orchids are such great houseplants that it's worth knowing what they like in terms of care so that you can keep them for ever, rather than chucking them out and buying new ones every year. Even though they're rather ubiquitous now, and have lost some of their mystique as a result, I still love the milky-white, rather sterile (unscented) purity of these plants. A line of three or five on a table has the power to bestow that calming, controlled, pared-down hip-hotel-like chic that we all love so much, though now I'm more likely to cut the flowers off and put them in my hair – a form of decadence which is afforded by being safe in the knowledge that there are plenty more. Here's how it's done.

THE LOWDOWN *Phalaenopsis* orchids are found in forests in the Himalayas, South East Asia and Northern Australia and are mostly epiphytes (i.e. they live up trees and have fleshy roots which get water from the moist air around them). The roots also photosynthesise and that's why they're often sold in white or clear pots so that the roots can get as much light as possible. The compost used is also very loose and made of bark chippings, again mimicking the kind of conditions you might get in a tree. They do really well in our heated homes because they like to be warm, and have adapted to the low light levels found in forests.

The plant you buy will have the capacity to flower intermittently all year round if you follow these simple rules:

Light Grow it away from direct sunlight – a west- or east-facing window is great, but otherwise the centre of a room.

Temperature Central heating is fine (orchids can deal with up to 30 degrees by day), but it's good for your orchid – and for you – to have it lower or switched off at night. Keep night temperatures no lower than 15 degrees.

Humidity It's really easy to give a plant humidity: just position the pot on top of a saucer or tray filled with pebbles or gravel and a little water, and top it up as it evaporates. Make sure the pot is kept above the water by the pebbles. This way you will create a humid microclimate around your plant and this will make it very happy.

Watering and feeding Keep it moist at all times but never wet. This means watering it once a week during summer and once a fortnight in winter. Use filtered water at room temperature (cold water will shock it). I fill a watering can the night before and use it the following morning. To water, take your plant to the sink and water the barky compost, letting it drain out of the pot. Feed the plant once a month (that's every fourth watering in summer, and every other in winter) using orchid fertiliser (available from garden centres) mixed with the water according to the instructions.

Rest If you want your plant to perform really, really well, put it into an unheated room (I use my loo) for a month to six weeks in autumn.

New compost Every three years or so, take the plant out of its pot and shake off the compost gently, and replace it with new orchid compost (available by mail order and from good nurseries).

Re-potting Orchids like being squashed, so you shouldn't need to re-pot again until growth appears to suffer (three or four years). Then you need to buy a larger clear or white plastic pot and re-pot your plant in it.

If you're feeling brave, cut the flower spike just above where the first flower appeared and it might produce another branch. In any case, cut all flower spikes at the base when the flowers are over and the spike has withered.

Roses

Most of us who are lucky enough to have some outside space have either planted or inherited a rose of some description. There are over 150 species of rose, and hundreds of different roses that belong to each, and although they are all recognisable as roses, the properties of some groups differ wildly from others, as do our tastes and preferences. It's all quite confusing for a virgin, and the investigation is a project in itself.

Here I have set down all the things I wanted to know about roses but had to wade through a mountain of conflicting information to get. I have shed some light on the jargon surrounding different roses, and demystified all the stuff involved with their upkeep, so that you can get on with the delicious job of choosing, growing and enjoying them.

THE LOWDOWN Roses have been so popular through history that they have been endlessly mucked about with in terms of hybridisation. This has given rise to different categories, each with its own desperately romantic name. Here are the groups:

Rose species These are the wild roses from which all the others originate. They have simple, single flowers in early summer and are very variable.

Old roses Sometimes called Old-fashioned, Antique, Heritage or Historic. The name means that they were all introduced into this country before a certain date. Some say 1867, some say 1945 – people still fight about it. Old roses look 'old': they remind you of seventeenth-century Dutch paintings and the Empress Josephine – exquisitely romantic. This group contains the roses with names that make you want to eat them, like Damask, Moss, Noisette, Damask Portland, Boursault and Centifolia. They are all different and all beautiful, but often (not always) flower only once and are prone to some diseases. These are the roses from which modern roses are bred.

Modern roses This group contains the Hybrid Teas. They have a distinctly different allure to the old roses, with large flowers on long upright stems that are perfect for cutting, and they are therefore grown in vast quantities for the commercial cut-flower market. They are really healthy, come in every conceivable colour except blue and mostly scented. This is the rose you get from the petrol station, and whilst it doesn't have the romance of an old rose, it has given rise in part to the birth of many cultivars that are not only exquisitely beautiful but also possess its health and vigour. Also in this group are the Climbing roses, Floribundas (with clusters of flowers), Miniature and Patio roses, Polyantha, Rambler and Rugosa roses.

Rose breeders are creating new roses all the time, with the emphasis on disease resistance, remontancy (repeat flowering), colour, form, hardiness and scent. Some like David Austin have devoted themselves to getting all this together with the gorgeous look of the old roses. His efforts have been a success, resulting in the English Roses. The point I am making is that unlike some things, the old originals are not necessarily the best option, so if you are captivated by old roses (as I am), it is possible to get that look and have repeat-flowering and disease-resistance … It's just a question of going shopping (see Suppliers, page 262).

The main thing is to know that there is a rose for every possible situation – including things like shade and areas with winters that are sub-zero – so ask the supplier to advise you. They adore doing this – it's their thing.

CARING FOR ROSES   People think this is complicated. It is not. Roses are mostly fully hardy and very tough. An established rose is difficult to kill; even if you chop it right down it will often re-grow. There are things you can do to make them extra comfortable and therefore better performers. Here are those things.

❈   Most roses want an open site in full sun.

❈   They like well-drained soil that is humus-rich. This means that they adore being given some well-rotted manure or similar to keep the ground moist and weed free (see page 227 for information on mulching).

❈   They like being fed. You can get rose fertiliser in granular or liquid form from any garden centre. You should give them this in the growing season, following the instructions on the packet.

❈   Established roses do not need watering unless it is very hot and dry in summer. Newly planted roses, though, need watering to become established.

❈   If you remove the spent flowers on a rose (deadheading), the plant will concentrate its energy on producing more.

❈   Most roses respond well to pruning, which is really easy if you let your instinct guide you. For more on pruning, see page 232.

PESTS AND DISEASES   Some roses are more susceptible than others. For common pests and diseases and methods of control, see pages 239 and 243–4.

If you want to spray (and you may easily, because it's just heartbreaking to see those little buds covered in aphids and blackspot), use something like Roseclear every two weeks from the beginning of March until late June. (Always, always follow the instructions on the bottle, and try to spray early in the morning and when the breeze is at its lowest so that you don't harm too many beneficial bugs in the process.) You may also wish to alternate between one type of spray and another, because after a while the little suckers become immune.

The absolute best way to combat these problems, though, is to go out there every day and squish the aphids, and pick off any leaves affected with blackspot and burn them whenever you have a spare five minutes.

How to make compost

Not so very long ago a gardener friend of mine invited me to see her garden. She led the way through the door and out into the beautiful oasis that she had created. I stood on the terrace taking it all in, but she kept on walking, ignoring my oohs and aahs, right down to the bottom of her garden. There she presented to me what she called her 'pride and joy' — the compost heap. Gardeners are nutty about compost, and they are right to be: no amount of loving care and attention to your plants above ground can match the positive effects of a great growing medium (see page 226). It's the beginning of everything, and nothing works without it. Here's how to do it.

THE LOWDOWN

Common sense is the main ingredient with compost, along with a good dose of trial and error. There are a million ways to make it, and if you have the space it's one of the most rewarding things you can do. The basic science is this: organic waste material is broken down by welcome guests (bacteria, worms, insects, fungi), releasing nutrients. The composter's job is really just to keep these guests happy, and to do that you have to give them food, water and oxygen.

It's rather like baking a cake with two main ingredients: green, nitrogen-rich materials, and brown carbon-rich materials, which you add in roughly equal amounts and mix up to create something new. Organic matter is decomposing all the time — a compost heap is just a way of having lots of it all in one place, and upping the ante so that the process is as efficient as possible.

TIMING

Start in spring, because you'll have lots of material to add.

YOU WILL NEED

A compost bin Or use two if you have the space. These can sometimes be obtained from the local council; or you can buy them at pretty much any big DIY store. Like plants, they come in a plethora of forms. Some are better than others, but remember that it's your effort and care, not the bin, that will make great compost. Make sure whatever you get has a cover or lid. If you don't have an outside space, you can still make compost in your kitchen, as the wonderful Japanese do, in a Bokashi bin.
Stuff to go in it See suggestions below.

METHOD

Set up your bin or bins in a shady place and either put them directly on bare soil or line the bottom with twiggy things to provide ventilation and drainage. Now you are ready to fill it. To do this you can, in theory, use anything that has ever lived, animal or vegetable, but to start with, stick to ordinary garden material (but see below for exceptions) like weeds, prunings, fallen leaves and lawn clippings; manure, straw, newspaper, cardboard, and uncooked fruit and vegetable waste from the kitchen; droppings and bedding of small rodents, if you keep them as pets; and lastly, any worn-out clothes made of natural fabrics.

The most important thing is to make sure that everything is in small pieces, as this makes the best compost, so shred and tear and cut to your heart's content.

Do not, on any account, compost any of the following – doing so is counter-productive and will make you cross and disillusioned: perennial weeds (such as dandelions and bindweed . . . bad bad bad, because they will spring up when you come to use your compost later); annual weeds that have flowered (the seeds will survive); anything diseased or infested with soil pests like vine weevil; cooked food, meat, fish and anything that will encourage vermin (nasty); man-made fabrics; dog or cat poo (no matter how organically you feed your little darlings); and anything with thorns (you will want to caress your compost when it's ready).

The compost will be built up in layers, and each addition has its own properties. Keep the layers thin, or mix up the different materials beforehand.

Make sure that you do not add too much of one thing in one go. If, for example, you add a vast heap of grass mowings, which can easily become compacted, you'll end up with a layer of slime – this is not nice. If the compost seems very dry (which it shouldn't, if you've cut everything up small), add some water to get it going. It should be damp, but not wet. The truly organic often pee on their compost heaps.

What happens is that an army of micro-organisms will start working, producing heat and breaking down the material. This can take anything between two months and a year.

The more you mix your compost, the quicker it will break down. Some do this every two months; some wait till the bin is full. To do this you must remove the whole lot and make sure all the stuff on the sides is in the middle, and all the stuff on the top is at the bottom ... It's hard work, but will make better compost. Return the mixed compost to the bin and leave it to mature into something lovely and crumbly. If you have only one bin, you can start using the compost from the bottom of the heap (bought bins have a special hatch for this purpose) and keep adding to the top. If you have two bins, you can begin again in the second one whilst you are using the contents of the first.

Problems with compost require nothing more than common sense to put right. For example, if it's too wet, it probably means you have too much leafy, grassy stuff in there, so take it out and mix it thoroughly with dry stuff like shredded newspaper or cardboard. If it's too dry, do the opposite, and perhaps add some liquid. Compost should smell nice, not nasty, so if it's gipping, you've probably been neglectful and added cooked kitchen waste or too much wet stuff in one go – again, mix in drier stuff.

That's the basics, and you'll get lovely compost from the above. But compost, like plants, is a huge subject that's worth getting deeper into, so get Googling and join the revolution.

Kitchen sink cloning

Imagine if you cut off your own finger or toe, left it alone for a while and came back to find that a whole new you had sprouted from it. Plants do this on a regular basis in one way or another, and taking a leaf cutting from a Streptocarpus (cape primrose) is a lovely way to see it happen at close quarters. I adore doing this — it's fascinating.

THE LOWDOWN

Streptocarpus are a large genus of frost-tender annuals and perennials, from Africa, Madagascar and China. They like to hang out in damp, tropical places like rainforests. This makes them really good houseplants, because they can deal with low light levels. They have these tubular, lobed flowers, often veined and always velvety, that just keep coming and coming in the most obliging way, and lots of big, wrinkled hairy leaves.

You'll find them in the Houseplant section of garden centres. Perhaps because of their value as houseplants, these, along with African violets (*Saintpaulia*), have a massive following of dedicated specialists, so there are more than enough chatrooms to go to for support if this plant becomes an obsession.

TIMING

Do this in spring when the plant is growing strongly.

YOU WILL NEED

1 *Streptocarpus* leaf Nice and big and healthy. Cut it off the plant from the base. You can buy plants from the indoor section of garden centres, or see the suppliers list on page 262.
A shallow plastic tray A seed tray is best. Make sure it has drainage holes and that your leaf will fit into it lengthways.
Some seed and cuttings compost You can buy this ready-made in bags or make your own from any old multi-purpose mixed half and half with horticultural grit.
A propagator Or a plastic lid to fit over your seed tray, or a plastic bag.
A really sharp knife I use those surgical scalpels that you can buy with extra blades from art shops.

METHOD

Prepare your seed tray by creating a nice flat bed of gritty compost. Put the tray in another tray of water until the surface glistens and draw two shallow lines in it lengthways with a pencil to insert your cuttings in.

Now imagine you're a surgeon, and lay your leaf, underside up, on a clean surface and slice it cleanly either side of the big vein that runs along the middle. What you're doing here is wounding each of the veins that branch out from it, so that the cells in each one will get working to produce new plants — amazing. Throw away the midrib and push each half, cut side down, into the trench you've made, firming the compost around the cut on either side. The finished result should look like the fins of two green sea monsters.

Put the whole thing in the propagator or plastic bag and keep an eye on it to make sure it doesn't dry out. In a few weeks you will be amazed to see tiny new plants appearing all along the length of the leaf. Leave them for a few more weeks and then gently detach as many as you want, planting them carefully in individual pots of ordinary multi-purpose, where they will grow into clones of their parent.

Whether or not you're into cloning, the beauty of *Streptocarpus* means that this plant should be applied liberally to every house. Water them only when the compost has pretty much dried out, and feed them with something high in potash (like tomato fertiliser); or you can buy special *Streptocarpus* food in handy little 'pills' which you just push into the pot.

Lily pots for scent

Lilies are a real must-have for me, not just because one pot of lilies brought indoors can turn my entire flat into a pool of intoxicating scent but because they are so gratifyingly easy to grow. Buying lilies as cut flowers will seem a ridiculous extravagance once you've done this.

THE LOWDOWN

Lilies are bulbous plants that come in many permutations. The best one to start with is *Lilium regale*, the most forgiving of all, and perfect for a first-timer, although really any lily bulb that's sold at a garden centre or nursery will work. You'll need to pay attention to its eventual height, which will be listed on the packet, and buy your pots accordingly, as some lilies are very top heavy and pots can blow over if they're not sturdy enough.

TIMING

Plant your bulbs in March.

YOU WILL NEED

Lily bulbs I have new favourites every year, but the milky-white, heavily scented *Lilium* 'Casa Blanca' always steals my heart.
Compost I use a mixture of peat-free multi-purpose and John Innes No. 2.
A tall pot My lily pots measure roughly 30cm across and are 50cm deep. This size will be perfect for tall lilies (90cm–1m high).
Sharp sand
Osmacote granules (See page 229.) About one handful per pot.

METHOD

Mix up the compost with the Osmacote granules and fill the pot until you have about 15cm left to the rim. Now sprinkle in a handful of sharp sand, put the bulbs on top (I use three bulbs per pot) and bury them with more compost, leaving enough room at the top so that when you water it won't overflow. Water until it seeps out at the bottom of the pot, put it outside in a sunny spot and wait.

If you've chosen tall lilies, it's a good idea to put a pea stick (a thin wooden stick sold in florists and garden centres) next to each one to support it as it gets taller. You should have lilies in June for scented summer nights.

Lilies hate to be too wet, so wait until the compost is dry on top before each watering, and then water thoroughly. They also sometimes get attacked by bright red lily beetles, which have brown larvae covered in an odious poo-like substance – nasty … So squish them on sight.

AND MORE

Some lily stalks are strangely ugly, covered in lots of thin leaves that look like shaggy hair and remind me strangely of the Honey Monster. If you cut your lilies and bring them into the house, you can strip the leaves off, as florists do; but I often bring the whole pot inside and use twigs or contorted hazel stems stuck into the compost around the edge to screen off the stems.

When the flowers are over, either plunge the bulbs into a flowerbed or chuck them out (they will come back next year, but won't be as good). The outlay for buying lilies new each year is minimal compared to the vast sums they would cost at the florist.

Dahlias

These plants are simply the jolliest things you can have in your outside space, and they are brilliant for cutting, as they last for ages in a vase. But the best thing about them is that they can flower from July through to October.

THE LOWDOWN
Dahlias are tuberous perennials that come from Mexico and Central America and are therefore classified as tender in this country. If you live in a cold area, that means you should either treat them as an annual and chuck them at the end of the season, or lift and store the tubers. This used to be de rigueur for everyone, but trials have shown that in mild areas most of them survive over winter in the ground, if you cover them with a layer of mulch (see page 227). Dahlias need nice fertile soil and full sun, just as they get in Mexico, and you can grow them in pots or in the ground. Virgins should introduce themselves to this wonderful plant by using tubers from the garden centre.

TIMING
Late spring.

YOU WILL NEED
To go shopping Dahlias are beloved of many, many gardeners, so there are always loads in garden centres to choose from (and see below). Take note of their eventual height – you'll find this information on the packet. Do not be snobbish about mixing colours and shapes: the whole point of a dahlia is that it is deliciously over the top.
Fertile soil in full sun Or containers of your choice filled with multi-purpose compost.
Bamboo canes Or similar supports.

SOME OF MY FAVOURITE DAHLIAS
For pots (eventual height 60–75cm):
Dahlia **'Ellen Huston'** Burnt orange with deep maroon leaves.
D. **'Fascination'** Pink, double flowers with deep red leaves.
D. **'New Baby'** Small pompon orange balls of delight.
D. **'Roxy'** Shocking pink shot with crimson with blunt petals.

For the garden (eventual height 100cm or taller):
D. **'Hillcrest Royal'** Purple sea-urchin-type spikiness.
D. **'Sam Hopkins'** A black dahlia like no other.
D. **'Downham Royal'** or *D.* **'Hot Chocolate'** Neat little ball-shaped flowers in black.
D. coccinea A species (i.e. one of the originals) in perfect red.

METHOD
The easiest way to grow dahlias is to put them straight in the ground in late May (i.e. when frost is but a faint memory). Plant so that the top of the tuber is just below the surface of the soil and water them in well. If you want them to start flowering earlier, you can buy them in March or April and pot them up into plastic pots twice the size of the tuber with multi-purpose compost

and leave them in a frost-free place like a balcony or porch, watering them once a week after their initial watering-in, until the shoots come up. Then you can plant them out once there's no more risk of a frost.

Plant in pots in the same way, using your nice pots. Keep them in a frost-free place until it's warm enough to move them out into the open if you want.

Some dahlias get so tall that they need support to stay upright. For this, you can use a bamboo cane, or something similar.

Bear in mind that your dahlias, being so delicious, will attract all sorts of things that want to eat them. For advice on this, see page 239. I find tatty (i.e. eaten) petals a plus point, but realise that this may not be quite the thing for everyone.

AND MORE If you want a big dahlia arrangement, they need contrast, and for this I use something like acid-green euphorbia or the flowers of *Alchemilla mollis* (lady's mantle). On their own, I cut the stems short and pack them tightly into little vases, or float the flowers in shallow bowls.

Forcing daffodil bulbs for Christmas

Poinsettias are not the only Christmas plants. It is perfectly possible to eat Christmas lunch at a table heaving with lily-of-the-valley or tiny white daffodils. The fresh colour and scent created by forcing such plants are not only deeply chic but also shamefully easy to achieve, and provide a welcome break from the fuggy, spicy-sweet aromas associated with that time of year.

THE LOWDOWN   Prepared daffodil bulbs have been kept in cold storage by experts, tricking the plants into flowering early by simulating winter. These are sold under the name 'Paperwhite'. They are not hardy outdoors, so grow them in pots or bowls as described below. I suggest you grow lots, planting them in succession at weekly intervals if you want a continuous display. A room filled with many pots of one type of plant always looks fabulous.

TIMING   Most paperwhites take 8–9 weeks to flower from planting, so to get them out and on the table for Christmas Day you need to plant them up in mid to late October.

YOU WILL NEED   **Daffodil bulbs** Buy prepared bulbs: there are numerous different varieties, usually called 'Paperwhite' or 'Tazetta' in the shops. 'Ziva' is pure white and has a really strong scent. Either order these (lots of them) or buy from your local nursery (see Suppliers, page 262) and start planting as soon as you get them home. If you can't do this, store them in paper bags in an unheated room.
Containers You can use anything from ordinary shallow pots to old biscuit tins, depending on your taste. I use shallow terracotta pots, pretty china bowls or glass vases.
Compost or mulch Use bulb fibre, which you can buy in bags, ordinary multi-purpose compost or some kind of mulch – anything from gravel to marbles will work.

METHOD   If you are using compost or bulb fibre, make sure your containers have drainage holes, and fill the base with a layer of gravel, broken pieces of pot or broken-up polystyrene to provide proper drainage. There should be at least 10cm of compost or fibre under the bulbs, and the pointed tips should be level with the top of the pot. Cram in as many as will cover the surface, and cover with compost or fibre so that the tips peep out and there is a bit of room for watering. Water the whole thing thoroughly and place it in a cool bright frost-free place, such as near a window in an unheated room or on a sheltered balcony, and keep it watered so that it doesn't dry out.

     If you are using mulch, use containers without holes and put a layer of your marbles or gravel in the bottom so that when the bulbs are placed on top their tips are level with the top. Then put the bulbs in, fill in the gaps around them with more mulch and fill the whole thing with water up to the base of the bulbs. Put the container in a cool bright spot, and keep the water at this level.

You can prolong the life of the bulbs by moving them back to their cool place when you're not using them, but sometimes life is too short to be marching to and fro with pots, so just make sure you have lots of them on the go.

AND MORE   I often prepare one or three bulbs in a pretty bought glass or cup with modish white stones or those coloured glass chippings you can buy in bags and tie a bow round it – the perfect present for random aunts. This is also a rather good project for children to do if you have some bored ones knocking about.

Other bulbs or bulbous plants you can force for Christmas include hyacinths, tulips, lily-of-the-valley and the ever-present, glorious amaryllis.

Tulip favouritism

I have no room for many tulips and for once I'm OK with that – there is such a vast choice that I would be overwhelmed. Instead, I do the tulip thing on a really mini scale and choose three that I like – perhaps with different flowering times – and buy a few bulbs of each. I am always astonished by which one ends up stealing my heart. It's usually the one that looked the least promising: the one that seemed less exciting in the catalogues or on the packet. I love this game – it's taught me to linger longer over people, places and things whose wow-factor may not immediately be apparent. I have not been disappointed.

THE LOWDOWN
The depth of meaning that has been attached to this plant is astonishing. Tulips have caused humans to do really ridiculous things – read Anna Pavord or ask Wiki – but to grow them, all you need to know is that this is a hardy bulbous plant that comes in so many different permutations that all the brilliant classification geeks have split them up into smaller groups to make it easier for us to choose which ones we want. Names such as Single Early Group and Parrot Group give an idea of the look and flowering time, but tulips are so popular that it's unlikely you'll be buying or ordering without a photograph to seduce you.

Tulips come from a wide range of different places, but Central Asia and the Middle East are particularly tulip rich. Many of the outrageous and wonderful tulips you may want to grow have been bred by man, but it's a good idea to include at least one of the species tulips (wild forms) in your collection and perhaps you, like so many others, will be captivated by their simple charm.

This project is for planting in pots, but you can, of course, use any spare patch of ground as long as it is well drained.

TIMING
Plant your bulbs in November or December.

YOU WILL NEED
Tulip bulbs Bulb packets usually contain around six bulbs, although they are often sold 'pick 'n' mix' style, where you get a paper bag and choose your bulbs from open boxes. This way you can pick the biggest, firmest ones. (See Suppliers for mail-order details, page 262).
Pots I use a 20cm pot for three bulbs.
Peat-free multi-purpose compost or bulb fibre Special bulb fibre or compost is sold in bags.
Grit or sand
Mulch Use pea gravel or horticultural grit.

METHOD
Different tulips groups have different planting requirements, but as a general rule, all tulips hate excessive wetness, so sharply drained soil is a good idea – mix the compost with one-third grit or sand. Another general rule (for all bulbs) is to plant at twice the depth of the bulb, but read the instructions on the packet. Make sure you plant bulbs the right way up – the pointy bit is the top.

When you've covered them with compost, and pressed it gently down so that they're snug, put a layer of gravel over the top (squirrels like to bury their nuts inside pots like this during the winter and the gravel will deter them), water the whole thing well and put it outside, out of the way. The compost should be damp but never soggy, so keep an eye on it and water with care if it dries out. The tulips will begin to emerge in spring. Wait until they are fully grown and in bud before you bring them indoors to admire.

Keep them as cool as you can to prolong their indoor life (I sometimes put them outside for the night).

These tulips can be planted outside in the garden when they've finished flowering, although don't expect the same vibrant display until the bulbs have had a few years to bulk up. For this reason it's best to buy new bulbs every year if you're planting in pots.

MY FAVOURITE TULIPS (SO FAR)

Tulipa 'Abu Hassan' A Triumph tulip, flowering in April to early May. Deep velvety maroon fading to bright yellow at the top of the petals.

T. 'Prinses Irene' My first love: a single early which flowers early to mid-April. It is orange, with a soft purple flame – exquisite.

T. 'Queen of Night' A Single Late, flowering early to mid-May. This is the closest to a black tulip they've managed to get and possibly the sexiest thing on a stem.

T. 'Spring Green' A Viridiflora tulip which flowers early to late May and is white with a green stripe – deeply chic.

Species tulips (wild forms – smaller and more delicate):

T. acuminata Delicate pointed petals in red and yellow that look like flames. Flowers early to mid-spring.

T. kaufmanniana Early- to mid-spring-flowering tulip with flowers in many different colours that look like stars.

T. sprengeri Early summer-flowering little beauty with red or orange goblet flowers.

T. violacea Has starry purple flowers in early and mid-spring.

AND MORE

The smaller species tulips are great for presents, either in pots or baskets. Tulip flowers are also brilliant hiding places for small chocolate Easter eggs.

A bog in a bowl – carnivorous plants

Carnivorous plants are endlessly fascinating for adults and children alike, and their spookiness is heightened by their striking beauty. They are often placed in special places, where they can be examined close up, which makes people think they are difficult to look after, but this is not true.

THE LOWDOWN
These plants live in places where the soil is very low in nutrients. Because of this, they have had to adapt to eating insects and other things in order to get the good stuff that will help them grow. This means that in order to replicate their natural environment and keep them happy, you need to get hold of the appropriate growing medium, which (unfortunately) is moss peat, so unless you live in a bog, the trick is to think small.

TIMING
Spring.

YOU WILL NEED
Plants and compost You can buy carnivorous plants at all good nurseries, but none of them sells peat, so it's best to order some plants in a 'starter pack' from a specialist (see Suppliers, page 262) which will come complete with a little bag of growing medium, specially mixed so that it's perfect for your plants (see the suggestions overleaf). The other advantage of this is that you get to talk to someone who knows all about the plants they're selling. If you've already bought a plant from a garden centre, these people also sell suitable compost in small bags for when you want to re-pot it or use a larger container for a mixture of plants.

A container I use a shallow bowl measuring 30cm in diameter with a hole in the bottom.

Another container to act as a reservoir for water This goes underneath your plant pot. A shallower, wider bowl or one of those plastic pot saucers is great, so long as it is large enough for you to pour water into.

A supply of rainwater or a water filter This is absolutely essential. These plants will not tolerate tap water because it contains lime, which they hate. This is the reason why your little Venus fly trap keeled over and died. I keep a plastic tray outside to catch rainwater whenever it falls, but if I had a proper garden I'd install a water butt. I use this water for my bog, and my blueberries, and when I run out I use the water filter that I drink from.

METHOD
Remove the plants from their pots and put them in your container, filling in the gaps with special compost up to the same level as they were in their pots and firming them in gently. Put the bowl inside the water reservoir and add filtered water or rainwater to it, so that the plant container is sitting in about 3cm water. Keep this water topped up – remember that this is a bog, and bogs must be constantly soggy.

The site depends on what plants you have chosen, and check their hardiness, but most carnivorous plants (including the ones suggested below) are perfectly happy outside and in full sun. If you plan to keep the bog indoors that's fine, although keep the air flowing around them by having them near an open window whenever possible. Most of these plants need to go dormant in winter (including all the ones listed below), which means keeping them away from central heating when it starts to get cold and reducing the water so that the compost is just damp rather than soggy.

Greenfly like these plants and can be controlled by using something like Provado (see page 239). Remember good husbandry and remove any dead growth when you see it.

CARNIVOROUS
PLANTS TO TRY

Dionaea muscipula **(Venus fly trap)** Try if possible to avoid touching the little trigger hairs that make the trap shut, as this will wear out the plant if you do it too much, and don't feed it dead flies – you should let it catch its own food. This plant will flower, but if you want big traps you should remove the flowers.

Drosera **(sundew)** (See opposite.) Gorgeous jewel-like things, which have thin leaves with little hairs that secrete sticky globules of glue where insects get stuck, and which sparkle in the sun – a bowlful of these is a truly exquisite thing.

Sarracenia (See page 187.) Really striking tubular leaves, which trap flies by attracting them with sweet nectar around the edge. They then slip down and get digested in the tube. There are lots of hybrids and wonderful colours to choose from.

Luxuriate

I realised pretty early on in this game that some plants have an X-factor: that their allure for me cannot be assigned simply to beauty, scent, texture or movement – there is something more that hits the subconscious.

The fresh, lush smell of greenery … Well, it's more than just a smell: it's a damp, cool, buzzing 'aliveness' that hits the base of my brain and makes the little hairs on the back of my neck stand on end. The movement of certain plants when I breathe on them; watching the blind flailing tendrils of a climber as it seeks its next anchorage; the soporific, heavy-lidded giggly mood that takes over when a room is suffused with lavender; or simply plants that look silly and make people laugh – all these things come from the feeling of luxurious, absolute abundance that being surrounded by plants never fails to achieve.

The overall effect is one of private, secret comfort, either to revel in myself or to share with friends. I guess you might call it the ultimate state of relaxation.

Mossy pots

People complain about moss: moss on their lawn, moss in between the cracks in their paving stones, moss on their walls, moss on the tarmac ... The little man inside the Google is one of these people, assuming you are a moss-hater like him and providing you with a million ways to kill it. I, on the other hand, adore moss with a passion keen enough to make me want to read about such things as rhizoids and calyptras (or pixie caps). But that's only because I want to know how to provide the best conditions for these lovely soft-to-frizzy Zen-like hummocks of green so that I can have them around me all the time.

Some people make moss gardens in pots, with ferns and stones and little machines to simulate mist and fog, but I think moss is more beautiful on its own, treated as the main event. I aim one day to have enough space to make my own moss bed tucked away in a ferny glade for naked slumber under the stars in summertime ... For now, I content myself – and adorn my table – with mossy pots.

THE LOWDOWN

Mosses are found all over the world, often clinging to bare rocks in the searing sun or the most hostile of arctic and alpine environments. They belong to a group of plants called bryophytes and scientists reckon that they arose completely independently from the ancestral green algae that gave way to other plants way back in the primordial ooze.

They differ from other plants in that they don't have a root system as such, so they rely heavily on the atmosphere for their water supply. Some mosses have adapted in an extraordinary way to deal with drying out. They are able to survive for extended periods without water and then spring back to luscious life within minutes of getting a few drops. But if you want your moss soft and green, keep things damp and shady.

There are literally thousands of different types of moss, most of which don't even have common names.

TIMING

Any time.

SPHAGNUM MOSS

The moss you're most likely to see being sold in nurseries is sphagnum moss (bog or peat moss), which is generally sold in bags and used for lining hanging baskets and pots of bulbs to make them look pretty. If you use it, make sure the supplier is reputable, as there are criminals who steal it from unsustainable sites and you don't want to be encouraging them.

Sphagnum moss is amazing in that it establishes an acid pH that inhibits decomposition – hence the perfectly preserved ancient bodies with squashed faces in the British Museum which were discovered in bogs. This also makes it antiseptic and it was therefore used by MASH-type units in the First World War when they ran out of bandages – it soaked up blood and stopped wounds getting infected.

YOU WILL NEED   **Moss** Because moss grows in unlikely places, it is perfectly possible to collect it yourself rather than getting it from a nursery or garden centre. I often return home from tramping the streets with a pocketful of emerald softness pilfered from the base of a brick wall or street tree. Other people's gardens are great for this too (though always ask first).
Pots
Loam-based compost John Innes No. 2 is perfect.

METHOD   To make lots of mossy pots, just choose your pots, fill them with compost and pat it down firmly so it's compacted (this is important, as moss won't grow on loose airy soil). Now soak the compost until it's completely wet. It's important here to make sure the soil level is right, so that your moss will end up skimming the top of the pot, coming slightly proud of it – you don't want it obscured by the sides.

Then put your moss pieces on to the surface of the compost, creating a tapestry of different types or sticking to one sort, and press it down really firmly so that the water in the compost oozes up around your fingers (if I were making a moss garden outside I'd walk on it) – the most common cause of moss death is air pockets between moss and ground.

Keep the whole thing damp and outside in the shade, and bring in your little pots whenever you want them for decoration.

AND MORE   If you have a piece of moss you particularly love and want to propagate it, just rip a piece off and whiz it up in a blender with some water. Pour this over the surface of some fresh compost and you'll get new plants in about five weeks – no special treatment needed, except water.

Lavender for the under-80s

As with all good ideas, lavender and its uses have acquired a rather fuddy-duddy image over the years as its fans have grown older and younger generations have turned to more exotic scents. But this fantastic plant, with its heady aroma, is worth embracing, not just for its garden-worthiness but for the massive contribution it can make to the home. When I have a party at any time of year, there is always dried lavender all over the floor, for people to crush with their shoes, and the scent is, I promise you, a world away from any evocation of grannies knitting in rocking chairs. Lavender is sexy, so use it with abandon.

THE LOWDOWN

There are about 25 different species of *Lavandula*, which are evergreen shrubs originating from the Mediterranean to Asia and India. What they all have in common is that they grow in dry, exposed rocky places, so by definition, they are really tough plants and you can treat them mean. My favourites are *L. angustifolia* (often called English lavender), which is perfect for drying; *L. dentata*, which has beautiful, scalloped, deeply aromatic leaves; and *L. stoechas* (French lavender), which has prominent bracts like rabbit ears at the top of the flower stalks. Different varieties have flower colours ranging from purple to pink to white, so buy the plants in flower to get your favourite.

If you're planting lavender in the garden (and it makes a wonderful low hedge for edging a border), do so in spring and make sure your site is sunny and your soil is well drained. Keep it compact by clipping it in early or mid-spring. When you chop, make sure you don't cut into the woody bits at the base, because it won't regenerate if you do.

Lavender looks great in pots either grouped en masse in one area or on steps. I bring pots of it indoors to scent my flat. Buy plants from a good garden centre or nursery and re-pot them in terracotta pots in a loam-based potting compost such as John Innes No. 2.

HARVESTING AND DRYING LAVENDER

Harvest lavender as soon as it starts flowering in mid- to late summer. You don't have to wait until all the flowers are open, and go mad, because the more you cut it, the bushier the plant will get. Do this on a dry day before noon, so that you get the best scent.

To dry the flowers, tie the stalks up in small bunches and hang them upside down somewhere warmish and airy, preferably in the dark so that they keep their colour. I often hang mine with the flowerheads in a paper bag. The job will be done in about a week.

LIVING WITH LAVENDER

At this point my head is full of grand plans for elaborate pot pourris, which invariably never come to fruition. Here are some of the ways in which I use my dried bunches *and* live my life.

❋ Strip the flowers from their stalks and scatter them wherever you want scent. Heat is a great activator, so I often sprinkle flowers around candles on the table. The scent is a relaxation aid, and a fabulous way of de-stressing your guests after a busy working week.

❋ Hang or place bunches near a fire in winter.

❋ Cut stalks short and put them in little vases en masse – little vases, grouped together with dried lavender in them look gorgeous, whereas large arrangements of dried flowers are frankly just nasty.

❋ Crush the dried flowers and use them as you would other dried herbs. I sprinkle lavender on all manner of roasted meats and vegetables, and also in salad dressings.

❋ Make lavender butter by adding a couple of teaspoons of crushed dried lavender flowers, a bit of dried thyme and a squeeze of lemon juice to some softened unsalted butter. Whiz it up and refrigerate or freeze it until you want to use it.

❋ I make lavender bags, using any scraps of fabric I have and sewing up three sides of a little square, stuffing the 'pocket' with dried lavender and tying the top up at the neck with ribbon, like a sack. These are lovely, easy presents if you feel like getting creative, particularly for girls (and most of all if you give a pair of silk knickers with them). They are great moth deterrents too, so put one in every drawer or shelf in your cupboard.

AND MORE   If your lavender is flowering sparsely, or not flowering at all, it's probably because you're being too kind to it. Plants flower to reproduce, and they won't bother if they don't think their days are numbered, so once you have watered in a new plant, it should be left to its own devices (unless it is in a pot, in which case it will need regular watering). Most importantly, remember that the soil needs to be poor.

An April seduction

Feeling frisky? Got an empty pot? Ladies and gentlemen, I give you the exquisite Epimedium. This plant is said to be an aphrodisiac — and yes, it would indeed be a very special man who put a pot of Epimedium in flower between me and him on a spring evening.

Nothing, but nothing can match the understated, airy loveliness of this plant. It's essentially a mass of heart-shaped (but not obviously heart-shaped) leaves that stay gorgeous all year round, clothing the earth in billowing clouds; and as if that weren't enough, it throws up tiny spurred flowers on wiry, almost invisible stems like little butterflies that waft about with the slightest breath or sigh or giggle — flowers that laugh at your jokes and make you feel good.

THE LOWDOWN — *Epimediums* are evergreen and deciduous perennials that come from woodland and other shady places everywhere from the Mediterranean to temperate Eastern Asia. That means that when grown outdoors most can cope with areas where other things will not grow, like the dry shady places underneath shrubs and trees – bliss. They have lots of common names, from the rather scathing barrenwort to horny goatweed, which I like much better and makes me feel, well, sort of goatishly horny – so if you want to seduce someone during the months of April and May …

TIMING — Spring to early summer.

YOU WILL NEED — **1 *Epimedium* plant** Available from good garden centres and nurseries. There are many to choose from, with different-coloured flowers, different (dazzling) autumn leaf colour, different ultimate height, etc. They are all beautiful – do not agonise. If you can't decide, just buy lots.

1 pot for your plant Take into account that your plant will eventually want to spread out, but don't worry too much because it grows very slowly. More important is that your pot should be of the shallow variety, because you want to look at your date through the *Epimedium*. Alternatively, forget the planting and put your bought plant inside another container to hide its plastic, and go and make yourself look fabulous.

Some compost I use multi-purpose with a few handfuls of John Innes No. 2.

METHOD — Plant your *Epimedium* snugly in its new pot, and place it on a table between you and your companion. The rest should come naturally.

AND MORE — *Epimediums* are a wonderful way to avoid that bare look around spring bulbs, as the bulbs will come up through them.

They look breathtaking with ferns and other foliage textures.

If you've got really tiny weeny receptacles, like those test-tube vases or an old glass inkwell, a single stem of flowers by a bed is beautiful.

A scented indoor vine

I am nuts about this plant. It gives out the kind of scent that's so heady it's almost indecent. It starts flowering in May with little pink-flushed fleshy blooms that seem to go on and on. I have it by a window in my stairwell and it makes people linger there, sniffing the air, so that by the time they get to me at the top of the stairs they are suitably blissed out, perhaps even giggling without really knowing why — and that is how I like to be greeted. Find one if you possibly can and let it grow around a window.

THE LOWDOWN
Dregea sinensis, also known (fabulously) as Wattakaka, is a twining woody evergreen climber that comes from tropical forests in China. Although it is evergreen in the tropics, my plant sometimes loses all but one or two of its leaves in winter, only to sprout obligingly come springtime. I have it in a 20cm pot, and if I had room on the window ledge I'd put it in a bigger one; however, it doesn't seem to mind at all.

TIMING
Plant your vine in spring.

YOU WILL NEED
1 ***Dregea sinensis* plant** Look online or go to a good nursery.
1 pot, 20cm in diameter or larger
John Innes No. 2 compost
A handful of slow-release fertiliser for the first year
Some teacup hooks or other means of support
A sunny window

METHOD
Plant your vine carefully in the compost, having mixed the compost with the fertiliser granules in the pot, and gently teasing out the roots if the plant is pot bound. Firm it in well and water thoroughly. Place the pot by a window and screw in a hook to support the twining stems. Keep the vine watered and screw another hook into the window frame as and when needed. The effect should be one of barely contained wildness, so let the tendrils romp away and do their stuff, even if it means brushing them as you walk past. That's it: do nothing except keep it watered whilst it's growing and then reduce the watering in winter. Although the vine may be bare, it will still be whippy and pretty and absolutely nothing to be ashamed of.

Chillies

I am one of those rather babyish people who will always prefer the taste of something mild over anything that packs too much of a punch in the heat stakes, so I don't grow chillies for my own consumption — well, not physical anyway — but they are, in a sense, a plant to feed the soul. There is something inherently rather silly about a chilli, with its weird shapes and bright colours, and this is augmented by the fact that they take themselves seriously enough to be really fiery with it — very Scrappy-Doo, and it makes me laugh. And laughter (as we all know) makes the little fluffy pleasure cells explode in our heads (which is the same thing that happens when we have chocolate, sex … or chillies). They're lovely and easy to grow — have fun.

THE LOWDOWN

Chillies (*Capsicum*) are short-lived perennials, and you can find them in a range of varieties. They come from forest margins in tropical North and South America, so they don't like frost. They can be found in little pots in garden centres and nurseries, and these are great, but it's really easy and a lot cheaper to grow them from seed. If you stick to the dwarf cultivars, you can end up with lots of cheerful pots that are perfect for decoration, both indoors and out, and they have the added bonus of giving you a crop of peppers with which to make relish (perfect Christmas present). This project is for pots of chillies, but you could also grow them outside in a sunny spot with rich, well-drained soil.

TIMING

Sow the seeds in February.

YOU WILL NEED

Chilli seed Go for F1 hybrids such as 'Apache', which will give good results and therefore make you happier. (An F1 hybrid is the result of crossing specially selected plants very carefully, and produces plants that are stronger and more prolific. Because of this the seeds are always a little more expensive.) Make sure they're dwarfing or patio varieties. The seeds are available at good garden centres (or see seed suppliers on page 262).
Pots of various sizes See Method. Terracotta looks best.
Seed compost
Multi-purpose potting compost
Tomato fertiliser

METHOD

Sow the seeds in individual little pots under ½cm of sieved seed compost, water them and put into a heated propagator or in a tray on a windowsill with a lid on or in a plastic bag until they germinate and seedlings appear. At this point remove them from the propagator and put them on a windowsill, keeping them watered until you think they are big enough to be moved into larger pots.

There are no hard and fast rules here, but a good sign that something needs potting on is when you can see its roots appearing out of the bottom of its pot. Put it into a larger pot with a good multi-purpose compost (I use 20cm

pots for 'Apache' F1), taking care not to disturb it too much, water it in well and stick it by an open window, closing it at night, when it's nice and warm outside (i.e. not until May or June). After about a week or so of this treatment, the plant will be 'hardened off' and ready to go outside for the summer.

The plant should be fed when it starts to fruit, with some tomato food mixed into the watering can according to dilution instructions – every two weeks is fine. It's very important to keep this plant watered but not sopping wet: it needs to be kept moist in order to produce the fruits, so if you go on holiday, get someone to water your pots for you.

The peppers usually start off green and then turn red or orange, or whatever colour they want to be. To get lots of chillies, pick the fruit when it's still green, which will encourage the plant to start again and produce more fruit. Store the green chillies in a dry place and they will ripen. I pick from my plants until about September, and then I leave them to be decorative.

A water garden

My water garden represents the ultimate example of living within my means. The concept was simple: merely a river running through the bottom of my garden, a few frolicking salmon, the odd swimming-pool-sized pond and one or two large waterfalls … I got over it, and instead I have something that took me less than an hour to put together and which gives me more pleasure than I am prepared to bore you with. The point is that you can have a pond on your balcony or anywhere you have the space to put a container full of water.

THE LOWDOWN
There's no funny business with pumps and fountains involved here: my water garden is just a container filled with water and a few plants that like having wet feet. Aquatic plants are generally split up into categories depending on how deep they like to be. The category that serves this project is 'marginal plants', which live partially submerged at the water's edge in their natural environment. There is a vast range of them to choose from and they usually have their own section in good nurseries, where you will see them displayed, their pots submerged in shallow troughs full of water.

MY FAVOURITES
All these marginal plants are very happy to live under water in the shallows.

Butomus umbellatus (**flowering rush**) Tall rush-like thing with sweet-smelling pink flowers in summer.
Cyperus papyrus (**papyrus**), *C. alternifolius* (**umbrella plant**), *C. isocladus* (**dwarf papyrus**) Gorgeous greenery on elegant stems with firework-like delicate flowers from summer to autumn. These are not hardy and in winter need to be brought indoors.
Hydrocotyle sibthorpioides (**pennywort**) Makes an utterly beautiful carpet of leaves that will spill over the edge of the container. Try to find 'Crystal Confetti', which is variegated and sublime: if I were only allowed one marginal, it would be this one.
Iris pseudacorus '**Variegata**' (**variegated yellow flag iris**) A yellow iris of extreme gorgeosity, with variegated, sword-like leaves. It flowers in late summer. Lots of irises love to live as marginals, so this is not your only option.
Juncus ensifolius Looks like a miniature bullrush.
Lindernia grandiflora Low creeping thing with tiny purple flowers in summer. Not hardy in winter, so take it inside before the frost arrives.
Mimulus ringens (**Allegheny monkey musk**) Tall perennial with purple flowers in summer.
Myosotis scorpioides (**water forget-me-not**) Just like an ordinary forget-me-not, but in your pool. Bright blue flowers in early summer.
Myriophyllum aquaticum (**diamond milfoil or parrot feather**) Sometimes sold under the name *M. brasiliense*. Exquisite feathery green foliage that seems to want to escape. A good oxygenator.
Ranunculus flammula (**lesser spearwort**) A water buttercup with bright yellow flowers in summer, and a British native plant.

TIMING	Spring to summer.
YOU WILL NEED	**A water-tight container** If you want to start small, a large china bowl is great for one or two plants, as long as it is wide and deep enough to hold them, with room for the water level to come above the pots at the appropriate level (see below). A half-barrel is an ideal vessel (lined, of course), or an old tin bath, the sort people used for their annual wash in front of the fire before bathrooms existed.
	Some marginal plants Choose your plants (see above, and Suppliers, page 262) only when you have your container. There are so many (see my favourites above) that you positively need to have some restrictions. Each plant will have a depth requirement, indicating how high the water must come over the top of soil in the pot for it to flourish. Think about having different heights and textures, and make sure you choose at least one oxygenating plant to keep the water clean.
	A few bricks and stones These are to create platforms inside your container so that each plant can stand at its perfect depth.
METHOD	Approach this as if you are doing a puzzle, and have some fun arranging your plants inside their pots in the container. Use the bricks underneath pots to raise them up, and around them to wedge them firmly in place. Low-growing, creeping plants are lovely around the edge, with taller, more architectural ones in the centre or at the back. Now simply fill the whole thing up with ordinary water and watch all the pots disappear – your bath is ready.
	Keep the water topped up – it's amazing how quickly it evaporates – and if you have bought plants that won't make it through the winter, remember which ones they are and take them inside for the winter months, where they can live in a spare bowl by a window. All these plants will eventually grow and the place will get crowded. It's best to watch them as they grow and find out which ones you really love, and then delve a little deeper into how to care for them (some will want pruning, re-potting, dividing, etc.).
AND MORE	A small pot of pennywort or milfoil or *Lindernia* is beautiful placed inside a bowl and brought to the table for decoration.

A glorious summer vine

This is my absolute favourite plant for instant gratification in the summer. Its lack of any discernible scent is more than made up for by the big coffee-cup, bell-like flowers with curly-whirly tendrils and saucer-like calyces (outer leaves), which stay on the vine so prettily long after the actual flowers have gone. I have always grown it outside, straight from seed (which makes it doubly satisfying), but will be trying it this year indoors, treating it as a permanent fixture rather than an annual feature to get rid of when it's past its best. You can grow it anywhere, as long as there's something for it to scramble up and over, like a wall.

The tendrils are amazing, in that they have a sort of rubbery stickiness to them and wave around, attaching themselves to anything, eventually gaining purchase and coiling up to anchor the plant to the surface. This thing can get really big, so make sure that the area to be covered is low enough that you'll be able to see the flowers.

The flowers are really long lasting as cut blooms. They go through various stages of growth as each one flowers (see opposite) and they look beautiful in low bowls or in small bud vases dotted around the room. They are also strong enough to withstand a day's work in your hair or buttonhole if you so desire. Not bad for a wrinkly little shrivelled-up seed.

THE LOWDOWN
Cobaea scandens (the cup and saucer vine) is actually a semi-evergreen climber when it's at home (which is in forest thickets in Mexico), but in this country it's started again every year from seed because it's frost-tender and looks better when it's grown fresh. You'll be pleased to know that it comes in two colours: white and purple. I like purple, but white is very chic.

TIMING
Start the seeds in February or March.

YOU WILL NEED
A packet of *Cobaea scandens* seeds Available online (see Suppliers, page 262).
Some pots See Method.
Gritty seed compost
Multi-purpose compost and John Innes No. 2
Something for the plants to climb up A wall or trellis, for example.

METHOD
Soak the seeds overnight in lukewarm water and plant them, one to a little pot, about 1cm deep in some gritty compost. Water them well and place either in a propagator or on a warm windowsill covered with a plastic bag. They will germinate quickly, at which time you should remove them from the propagator or take off the plastic bag and keep them growing on indoors until the last frost of the year has gone. Give them a spell by an open window for about a week, before planting them in larger pots. Water them in and let them romp up walls, along trellises, around obelisks and generally everywhere you allow them to (and some places you don't). You can also plant them straight into the ground at the base of a wall or something supportive. This plant will keep bearing its fabulous blooms all summer and most of the autumn long.

Grow your own pineapples

It may seem a wild idea, but in fact the only requirements for growing your own pineapples are a sunny windowsill and the ability to fill a watering can. I'm not saying you'll get supermarket-sized fruit, but you won't get no fruit, and you'll get to watch something appear miraculously out of nothing.

THE LOWDOWN

Despite being commercially grown in Hawaii and very much associated with that place, the pineapple we are used to (*Ananas comosus*) is a perennial and comes from Brazil, and is therefore frost-tender. Pineapples are bromeliads, and this one is a terrestrial bromeliad, which means it likes to hang out on the ground – and that means that you and I can grow it in a pot.

TIMING

Spring.

YOU WILL NEED

A delicious pineapple Buy this from the supermarket – preferably a fruit that's just about to ripen.
A thick pair of gloves
A big sharp knife
A terracotta pot roughly 20cm diameter
Some multi-purpose compost mixed with grit, or bromeliad compost

METHOD

Take your gloves, grasp the prickly leaves firmly and twist the crown out of the main fruit. Then make a pineapple upside-down cake (this just-under-ripe pineapple may not be sweet enough to enjoy as is) from the main fruit and keep the crown.

Ensure you get rid of any fruit attached to the crown, strip a few leaves off the bottom part of the crown to make a stem for planting in the soil, and start cutting thin slices off it, until you can see little circles in the cut surface. These are root buds. Stop cutting as soon this happens and set the whole thing aside for a few days (up to a week is fine) in order for the wound to callous over. This will prevent rotting.

When this is done, stick the stem into your pot, filled with compost. You want to keep the soil barely moist, so water once a week and no more, misting the leaves at the same time, and stop all watering in late autumn right through to mid-spring. You can put the plant outside in summer, but keep it away from direct scorching sunlight, which will burn it. In the second or third year, the plant will flower, and then fruit, but if you want to try to force it, here's how.

Ethylene is a gas produced naturally by fruits, which induces flowering and ripening. Manufacturers manipulate nature by cutting off oxygen from harvested unripe fruits, inhibiting the formation of ethylene. This is the fruit equivalent of cryogenics, keeping them in a suspended state where time has no effect – spooky, but convenient, as it means the farmers can remove the fruit from this environment in batches, which will then ripen. In this way they give us just-ripe fruit all year round.

You can use apples to force your pineapple into fruit by putting the plant inside a plastic bag with some ripe ones and leaving it for a couple of weeks. The rotting apples will give off enough ethylene to discourage leaf formation and encourage flowering. The fruit will be small, but geeks eat Milky Bars, not pineapples.

AND MORE   If you get into the idea of growing bigger, better pineapples, use the side-shoots that your plant will probably throw out. Cut these off and plant them in separate pots, keeping them really warm at the roots (you could fashion some kind of stand over your radiator or something) and keep potting the plant up in spring into a larger pot (in the wild, this plant would be about 1m high).

A night-scented bower

When this virgin started gardening not so very long ago she amassed a small collection of plants that were not only beautiful but famed for their evening scent. She put them on her balcony and experienced for the first time the exquisite pleasure to be had from stealing away in the darkness and getting thoroughly intoxicated.

Everyone should do this. It doesn't matter how small or large the space, whether you're alone or with friends — there is no better way to spend a summer night. Oh, and if you can lure a potential lover into your scented bower, just make sure you're ready for anything from ravishment to marriage proposals — you have been warned ...

THE LOWDOWN Although we might be forgiven for thinking that night-scented plants are there purely for our pleasure, the truth is that the pleasure they give us is actually just a happy by-product of their reproductive drive. These plants generally rely on pollinators such as moths and bats, who come out at night to get their sweet treats. For this reason many of the plants in this category have pale or white flowers that glow in the dark, but rely primarily on the heady scent they give out to attract their unwitting sex slaves.

In my experience it is best to concentrate on one or two scents in a small area rather than lots. All the suggestions below are widely available and can be planted in the ground or in pots and brought indoors whenever you want to create midnight madness.

MY FAVOURITES **Gladiolus tristis** This is nothing like the Day-Glo-glorious gladioli grown for their massive blowsy blooms (though they're heavenly in their own way). This is a rather understated thing, with funnel-shaped flowers of palest yellow or creamy white, which comes from the Western Cape of South Africa and flowers in spring, producing an evening scent that will make you splay your toes. To grow this, you need to get on the Google and source some corms, which you bury 15cm deep in a pot of John Innes No. 1 compost. I plant them in spring, and put about ten in a 28cm pot, which is 25cm deep. They want a nice cushy life with lots of sun.

They flower in summer, and when they are over and the leaves have turned brown, you can lift them out of the soil and dry them out, and then store them over the winter somewhere unheated and frost free until next year (or do as I do and start again with new bulbs). Another gladiolus, *G. murielae* (sometimes called *Acidanthera* or *G. callianthus*), will provide you with the same pleasure in late summer, so get some of those too.

Matthiola longipetala subsp. bicornis (night-scented stock) This is sometimes sold under the name of *Matthiola bicornis*, and you can get the seeds anywhere or buy it as a plant when it's out in summer. It's an annual, and you'll want lots of it, so it's much cheaper to use seed. You can sow it outside in springtime either in pots of multi-purpose compost or in the ground in a spot with plenty of sun. I have it in window boxes and let the musky scent waft in on warm summer nights.

***Nicotiana* (tobacco plant)** Get either *N. alata* or *N. sylvestris* (see page 212). Although these plants, which come from Brazil and Argentina, are actually perennials, they are treated like annuals in this country because they get cross and sometimes die in winter (very off-putting for a virgin). Either buy a packet of seeds and sow them in mid-spring, or buy young plants when they hit the stands at garden centres. They have trumpet-shaped flowers in the summer with a heady floral scent in the evening. They can reach the dizzy heights of up to 1.5m, so you may need to stick a few canes in the ground or in your pots to secure them to. I grow them in pots 10cm apart, and I grow them from seed because a few are simply not enough. They want full sun to partial shade, which is what they get on the mountain slopes and valley floors of their native land.

A little meadow for private sunbathing

This is the easiest, quickest and most rewarding thing a virgin can do when faced with a spare patch of garden or even a leftover window box. Lots of 'real' gardeners sow annual wildflowers as a means of buying time whilst they work out what they really want to do with a new plot, as it gives spectacular results with hardly any effort.

THE LOWDOWN
First things first: the whole meadow thing is a real art, a delicate balance between man and nature maintained by carefully timed cutting and maintenance. This project is therefore not a real meadow, but simply the sowing of hardy annual wildflower seed to re-create the look of what used to happen in arable fields in days gone by. So although it's probably not strictly correct to call it a meadow, when I'm sitting in a patch of annual wildflowers, and I get butterflies and bees and a sunny day, that's meadowish enough for me.

TIMING
The best time to do this is in the autumn, because some plants need a cold spell in order to germinate – your seed packet will tell you more; but you can do it in spring (no later than March) as well.

YOU WILL NEED
A packet of wildflower seeds These are widely available and usually contain things like poppies and cornflowers and corncockles. The packet will tell you how much area the seeds will cover. It's a good thing to buy your seeds from wildlife charities, as they collect their seed from sustainable stocks.
A spare piece of ground As small or as big as you like.
A sunny site Think farmland, where there's very little shade.

METHOD
All you need to do is prepare the ground to achieve what gardeners refer to as a fine tilth. This basically means that you have broken up any clods of earth and raked over the entire area so that the surface is lovely and fine and crumbly – the sort of texture that would make it easy for a germinating seed to push its way up and out of.

Now make some patterns in the soil with a stick or your finger – such as big crosses or zigzags – and scatter your seeds as evenly and thinly as possible so that they fall roughly inside these furrows. Some people mix their seed with sand so that they can see where it has fallen. Then cover it all lightly and pat it down so that the seeds are in contact with the soil.

Once the seeds start growing in spring, you should keep an eye on your patch for weeds. Weed seedlings are not easy to distinguish from the plants you want to keep, but you will know roughly which are weeds because of the patterns you made. Don't worry about it not looking natural – it will.

AND MORE
If you love your meadow and want the same again next year, wait till the flowers are over and their seeds have fallen in late September, and then cut everything down. Dig over your patch the following spring, and you'll get the same again … and again … and again.

Jungle greens

A certain smugness is something to be encouraged when it comes to growing things, as it's usually born of deep self-satisfaction rather than a 'mine's better than yours' type of feeling. There are times when smugness is the only way to celebrate, particularly when it comes to saving money.

For me, the first time this happened was with a banana. Having grown four enormous beauteous paddle-leaved giants from seed, I happened to spy the same thing at my local garden centre being sold for the kind of money that made me blanch. These plants will grow almost in spite of you. I use them to green up my flat, and put them outside in the sun for a summer holiday. They need protection from cold weather (see page 235), which is why it is best to keep them in pots, as it's easier to move them to a sheltered spot. These are also the perfect seeds to sow with children, as the experience is a big one, in every way.

THE LOWDOWN
The Abyssinian banana (*Ensete ventricosum*) comes from the lower mountains of tropical Africa and Asia and is an evergreen perennial. This means that although it stops growing in the winter, it doesn't retreat underground, so you get the benefit of its massive lush green leaves all year round. It can cope with low indoor light levels because of its great big leaves. You can get it in two different colours: classic green or deep maroon (a variety called 'Maurelii').

TIMING
Spring.

YOU WILL NEED
Ensete ventricosum seeds These are available from most nurseries and online.
Small 6cm pots
Gritty seed compost
Pots and compost for potting up See Method.

METHOD
Soak the large seeds in tepid water for 24 hours and then put each one in a little pot filled with seed compost. Bury them about 1cm deep. Water them and either place in a propagator or cover the pots with a plastic bag secured with an elastic band. Keep them damp, humid and cosy. The seeds will germinate erratically, so don't give up on them if they're taking their time. The first time I did this, the first seedling appeared after a week, and the last one showed up four months later.

As soon as they appear, remove them from the propagator and give them as much light as possible. If it's mild outside, put them out, or place them near an open window in the daytime, but keep them away from direct sunlight, as you would any baby. When you can see roots coming out of the bottom of the little pot, move them to a bigger one, using richer loam-based compost (John Innes No. 2). Keep potting them on in this way until they're in large pots.

These plants are gratifyingly fast to grow and can grow 2m or more in a few months, depending on how happy they are. They add a lovely tropical feeling to any outside space, but for me it's all about sitting underneath them in my flip-flops drinking cocktails in the depths of winter.

Extras

The basics I have set down at the beginning of this book will give you all the information you need to start growing things. What follows are answers to some of the questions that will probably have arisen about gardening – both theoretical and practical – during the process (at least, they did with me) …

Plant names

Plant nomenclature is often a touchy subject, but as you get more interested you become aware that using their Latin names is the only way to be precise about what you're dealing with. The main reason for this is that Latin names are universal, whereas common names differ from region to region, and for some plants, there is no common name.

THE LOWDOWN   Latin names seem complicated at first, just as any foreign language does. Because of new research, particularly on a genetic level, these names also get changed from time to time, with plants being shunted around into different genera and families; no wonder, then, that people shy away from all this stuff. But using them actually makes things a lot easier in the long run, because the names often have descriptive parts to them (e.g. *fastigiata*, meaning upright), which means that you can get an idea of what the plant looks without seeing it.

Having said that, it was only from trusting others that Latin names were 'a good thing' that I eventually came to realise that they were right (books on nomenclature were no help at all: it was still all gobbledegook). So all I can say is that I am aided in my work by these names enough to make me really quite passionate about using them – and, being a lazy sort of person, I am not given to wasting my time with anything that doesn't make things easier or better. Besides which, Latin names are beautiful, which is a reason in itself.

The system was devised by a Swedish naturalist called Linnaeus. It's a binomial (two-name) system in which each plant name comprises a genus name and then a species name. After these come any varieties or subspecies (naturally occurring), and then any cultivars (varieties cultivated by man). It goes like this:

GENUS   A group of plants with features in common (the plural is genera).

SPECIES   Plants with specific individual characteristics within a genus.

VARIETY AND
SUBSPECIES   Plants within a species with an identifiable variation, such as flower colour. The variation has occurred naturally through the cross-fertilisation of plants. Abbreviated as var. or subsp.

CULTIVAR   A variety cultivated or perpetuated by man. The cultivar name is written next to the name in single quotation marks and usually in modern language, not Latin.

HYBRID   Plants that have arisen as a result of man's intervention and would not have happened in nature – often with parents from two or more different species.

At the top of this list come the plant families, which are not used as part of the name, but become more useful as you delve deeper into growing things. The family name is recognisable, as it always ends in the letters 'aceae'.

How plants grow – the science

Plant growth occurs when cells multiply and enlarge. To fuel this process, the plant needs energy, and that is why it photosynthesises, as follows.

The genius of a plant is the fact that it can harness and store light to help it make energy because its cells contain chlorophyll (the green pigment in leaves and stems). The chlorophyll absorbs the light. Plants use carbon dioxide from the air around them (the stuff that the rest of us produce as we breathe out) as the starting point for growing. They absorb carbon dioxide through pores in their leaves. When a plant gets carbon dioxide, and water, which it absorbs from the soil through its roots, it uses light to convert them into carbohydrate and oxygen. The plant turns the carbohydrate into sugar, the energy it needs to grow.

Here is the equation you learned at school but have now forgotten:
$$6CO_2 + 6H_2O \rightarrow C_6H_{12}O_6 + 6O_2$$

Or, in English:
carbon dioxide + water → carbohydrate + oxygen

The nutrients that a plant needs for healthy growth are present in soil. Therefore, put quite simply, if you give your plant soil, water it and keep it in a place where it gets enough light, you are giving it everything it needs.

Watering

The most frequently asked questions when it comes to growing things revolve around watering. The reason these questions are asked again and again is that there are so many answers, each plant having its ideal requirements of when, where and how much. Here is the universal answer to all these questions:

Find out where your plant comes from.

If you do this, you will be able to determine the climatic conditions it likes and either find out the area's precipitation rate (if you are so inclined) or make an educated guess as to how wet it likes to be.

I'm going to add to this some things about watering that I have learned from people who've been at it longer than I have:

1. If you are in any doubt, it is better to water than not.
2. It is very difficult to over-water as long as you have adequate drainage. For open ground, that means balanced soil structure (see soil types on page 227). For pots, it means having a hole or holes at the bottom.
3. It is always better to give a plant one good soaking than lots of little sprinklings. A good soaking encourages the roots to grow deep into the soil in search of moisture, also helping to anchor the plant into the ground. For newly planted shrubs in the open ground, use the contents of one or two large watering cans. For pots, water until you can see water coming out of the bottom.
4. Anything newly planted or moved should be watered in really well and watered regularly until it gets established.
5. If the top of the soil is dry, it doesn't necessarily mean the plant is thirsty. You do not have to use guesswork. Get your hand into the soil around the plant or down the side of the pot and feel how wet or dry it is below the surface.
6. A plant will generally let you know if it needs a drink by wilting. If you respond to this sign, it will probably be fine.

AND MORE   Placing trays or saucers underneath your pots will reduce the need for watering and give you an idea of how much the plant needs; it is really the only way to water properly, allowing the water to permeate the entire pot rather than just running straight through it. When you water pots, water will initially leach through the holes in the bottom. It will collect in the tray underneath the pot and then be taken up by the compost slowly by capillary action. You will know how much water your plant needs by noticing how many trays of water the plant takes up before it's had enough – it's likely to be so much more than you think. Once I realised this I began to pay much more attention to watering, and the plants thanked me for it.

Soil

Garden soil is simply a growing medium. Because of its structure, it provides a plant with a firm but penetrable base into which the plant can anchor itself with its roots. Soil also holds water and nutrients, which the plant can absorb through its roots.

If you have a garden, it is vital to remember that what you see above ground is less than half the story, and if you get that, you'll understand how important the growing medium is. If you become the slightest bit interested in your own garden soil (and you will, if you are at all interested in growing things), what you glean from a few simple investigations will open your eyes to why plants behave the way they do. And that means you'll end up with healthy luscious green stuff to be fantastically smug about.

WHAT'S GOING ON UNDERGROUND

The constituents of soil are 45 per cent mineral particles (sand, silt and clay) and 50 per cent air and water. The rest is made up of what is known as humus, or rotted organic matter (see below). The humus and mineral particles provide nutrients for plants. Then, of course, there are creepy crawlies (like worms) and plant roots.

The mineral particles in the soil are made from rock over long periods of time. The kinds your soil contains depends on the rock it is made from, and its pH value (see page 228).

The upper layer is called topsoil. This typically contains a much higher level of humus, plant nutrients and air (all things plant roots like). Underneath this is the subsoil, which is far less rich in organic matter and nutrients and should therefore stay where it is.

ORGANIC MATTER

This is the remains of plants and animals in various stages of decay. All organic matter breaks down slowly in the soil with the help of bacteria, fungi and worms. Essential nutrients are produced in this process and the volume of the decaying matter decreases. This is when you get humus.

Humus is really fabulous because it sticks to soil particles, making them into lovely crumbs, which in turn creates space for air and water. It also holds lots of water, and plant nutrients that would otherwise leach out, as well as feeding plants through the process of decay.

What I mean to say here is that there is no soil that the addition of humus will not improve. It will make sandy soil more fertile and water retentive, it will improve clay soil by binding the tiny particles into larger crumbs, improving drainage and aeration – and so on: to find out what soil you have and what to do about it, see the table opposite.

You can increase the amount of humus in your soil by adding bulky organic matter. This means manure or soil-improver, which you can buy in bags or beg from nearby animals; or you can make your own compost (see page 172). Each has its own merits, so experiment.

I do not dig organic matter into the soil unless I am desperate to do some really hard labour (rare). The idea of digging comes from a time when people had massive houses with lots and lots of staff who got very cold in the winter months. Getting them to dig kept them not only warm but extremely happy (boys love to dig holes). There is another reason not to dig, though, which is less facetious and lazy, and that is that if you churn up your soil with a spade, you are undoing all the good work that the worms have been hard at. They are the experts at mixing your soil. They incorporate organic matter beneath the surface by digesting it and burrowing down below to deposit it beneath by pooing it out (this poo is called wormcast and it is black gold), and they aerate the soil as they do this. So don't spoil their fun, or your soil, by digging – just keep adding organic matter on top.

MULCH   The term mulch is used for anything that you put on top of soil to stop water from evaporating or to suppress weeds; some mulches, like manure, leafmould or good garden compost, can also be a good way of adding nutrients to the soil, thus increasing its fertility, or protecting tender plants from the cold.

SOIL TYPES   To find out about your soil, all you have to do is to work with it a bit. You'll be able to distinguish its structure and then work out what to add in order to improve it. The ideal garden soil is a mixture of sand, clay and humus in proportions that make it both moisture retentive and well drained (yes, it is a paradox, but possible).

TYPE	DESCRIPTION	IMPROVEMENTS
Sandy	Large particles with big gaps between them. Light, easy to work. Very fast draining. Poor fertility, as nutrients are washed away.	Add organic matter every year. Mulch for water conservation. Feed plants.
Clay	Tiny particles which cake together. Heavy in winter, rock hard in summer. Slow draining. Rich in nutrients.	Add organic matter every year. Add sand or grit to break it up.
Loam	Mixture of clay and sand. Perfect drainage. Good fertility.	Add organic matter every few years.
Chalky	Crumbly soil with chalky bits. Often shallow and low in nutrients. Fast drainage.	Add organic matter whenever possible. Mulch for water conservation. Feed plants.
City soil	Often exhausted, low in nutrients. Either dusty or compacted.	Add organic matter regularly. Feed plants. Add sand, grit or soil-improver.

If your soil has lots of clay in it, you will be working with something that holds together when you squash it, and gets very hard in the summer and very cold and wet in the winter. Clay particles are really tiny (you need an electron microscope to see one) and because of this they all squidge together, so not much air and water can get in between them. This means that clay is slow to drain and prone to waterlogging. To make life better, you're going to need something to improve its structure by breaking it up – ideally sand.

The opposite is true of sandy soil (large particles mean poor moisture retention), to which you would ideally add clay – you get the picture. The table will give you an idea of what you can do to improve soil structure, which should be regarded as a long-term project.

SOIL PH Soil pH is a measure of its acidity or alkalinity – think school chemistry lessons with litmus paper (think hard). If you can't remember that, surely you remember those adverts for Dove soap?

While it is really worth the effort to improve the structure and texture of your soil, it's pretty crazy to try to change its pH (better to move house). So it is really useful to know your soil's pH, so that you can plant accordingly. If you're interested, get one of those pH testing kits from a garden centre and make like a CSI for half an hour. Then you'll have concrete evidence as to why, for instance, your rhododendron looks so miserable (rhododendrons like acid, not alkaline, soil). It will also save you time and money and make you feel good, as plants won't have to die because of your ignorance.

Having said that, unless your soil is very strongly acid or alkaline, with a whole range of plants it is worth experimenting, because plants want to grow, and most of them will find a way.

Feeding

The concept of 'feeding' a plant, to which entire sections of garden centres are dedicated, should really be seen as the supplementation of the plant's diet. As you grow as a plantsperson and become more aware of plants' individual nutrient requirements, you will find that supplementing their diet with essential nutrients produces healthier, more vigorous plants, and you may therefore wish to use plant food (or 'fertiliser'), particularly if you garden with pots. Technically, though, as long as you keep adding organic matter to your soil, none of this should be necessary.

All fertilisers are made up of varying degrees of the nutrients nitrogen, phosphorus and potassium. Here is what they do:

NUTRIENT	SYMBOL	FUNCTION
Nitrogen	N	Promotes leafy growth
Phosphorus	P	Promotes root growth
Potassium	K	Promotes flower and fruit growth

All packets of plant food have a list of the three main nutrient symbols (N, P and K), with numbers beside them to tell you what proportions they contain, so it is easy to tell what you are getting.

Fertilisers come in a variety of forms, used in different ways:

Granular fertiliser You measure this out and sprinkle it around the plant, mussing it into the top layer of soil.
Liquid fertiliser Easy for the plant to absorb, as you mix it with water.
Slow-release fertiliser, such as Osmacote Fertiliser that comes in little spherical balls and starts working when the soil warms up. It's great because it lasts for up to a year – particularly good for pots and lazy people.

I have a cupboard full of different bottles and packets, but the ones I use most often are liquid seaweed, which seems to do everything good, tomato fertiliser, which is high in potassium and therefore good for flowers and fruit, and Osmacote granules, which I mix with compost when I plant things. Always follow the instructions.

Husbandry

Watering is rule number one for keeping plants healthy (see page 225), but husbandry comes a close second. Clearing away dead stuff, deadheading and pinching out dead or withered bits will not only improve the look of the plant but keep it healthier too. It's a bit rich for me (someone who throws her clothes on the floor) to be saying this, but I do try to be tidy in when it comes to plants, because dead stuff can harbour all sorts of diseases and viruses if it's left hanging around — apart from which, you get the same sense of calm after you've swept away the debris as you do when you've folded all your clothes.

DEADHEADING
— THE SCIENCE

Plants have one obsession, and that is to reproduce. That's all they want to do, and one of the ways they do this is by producing seeds. Flowers only exist, from a plant's point of view, as a means of attracting pollinators (like bees), who visit them and transfer pollen on to them from another flower, which then fertilises that flower to make the seeds. When this has happened, the flower goes over: the petals wither and fall, and the flower forms a seedhead which swells, ready to drop the seeds on the ground, where they will grow into the next generation of plants. If, however, you come along and remove flowers (with their stalks) before or as they go over, you will trick the plant into making up for the loss of its potential to create seed by creating more flowers. Some plants will create flush after flush of flowers in this way, others give up the ghost after a couple of times. Either way, unless you specifically want the seedheads, it's always a good thing to deadhead flowers, if only to keep the plant looking gorgeous.

Pruning

The first thing to say about this is that you don't have to: plants will survive perfectly well without you lopping bits off them. But humans have discovered that pruning produces certain benefits to plants which in turn benefit them: namely, prolonging the life of the plant, keeping it within bounds, making it look better and encouraging it to produce more flowers or fruit. Pruning shouldn't be confused with trimming or clipping – it's more drastic than that, and therefore needs a few basic rules.

Before you start, here's the lowdown:

※ Think like a surgeon, and before you cut anything, make sure your equipment is clean and sharp, because hacking away at something with a dirty, blunt tool can leave it prone to disease.

※ Virgins should always prune in springtime. This is because pruning promotes new growth. New growth is delicate, and needs nice, warm weather to get it strong and ready for the winter, and springtime pruning gives the plant the longest stretch of cosiness possible, making it the least risky option.

※ Use common sense, remembering that plants are amazingly good at surviving – and always keep in mind that you are pruning to increase light and airflow.

BASIC RULES **The three Ds** Look for Dead, Diseased or Dying wood. Cut it out.
Think about shape If, for example, every time you walk outside you're battling through a thicket of thorny shoots that are making you wonder whether your tetanus jabs are up to date, this plant is outgrowing its space. Cut them off.
Crossing stems When shoots become mature and harden up, they can rub against each other if they're crossing. This injures the plant and leaves it prone to disease. Cut out the weakest one.

PRUNING LEVELS **Gentle pruning** It's unlikely you'll have to do this every year, because most candidates for this type of pruning are quite slow growing. Use the three basic rules above, along with your aesthetic sensibility and common sense.
Rejuvenating A little more drastic. When shrubs are left to themselves, growth on the outside stops light getting in to the centre, so inside there's just bare wood with no green. By pruning this out, you can invigorate the thing, and by allowing light to get through get more flowers and green. Get inside and follow the three basic rules above. You'll be left with something that looks rather odd at first but will soon fill out again. Remember not to wear your best clothes when you're messing around inside bushes.
Complete obliteration Or so it seems. Some plants respond to having the previous year's growth removed every year, at which stronger, healthier new growth will appear and take over. This means either cutting all the stems at

ground level, or cutting to within a few centimetres of the basic framework. It looks terrifying at first, but isn't.

AND MORE   Pruning is a fascinating business, and requirements for specific plants are outside the scope of this book. While pruning is certainly not as complicated as some people make it out to be, you can still kill a plant by doing it wrong, which is why it's always worth going online or opening a book to get the pruning lowdown on your particular plant before you start.

Frost protection

Some plants you will want to grow can't deal with frost. There are all sorts of ways to protect them without having to put up a greenhouse. All plants are different and the fact is that they often survive against all odds. The other thing worth knowing is that it sometimes doesn't fall below zero in many urban areas, so it's an idea to find out what the winter temperatures drop to in different parts of your space using a min/max thermometer (available at all good garden centres) — you could save yourself a lot of lifting and moving.

Bring plants indoors Anything frost-tender, like my banana plants, pelargoniums and papyrus, come indoors during the winter. I keep them near a window to give them as much light as possible.

Group pots together A huddle of plants near a wall will keep each other warm.

Keep pots off the ground with pot feet This will often stop non-frost-resistant pots from cracking.

Horticultural fleece This is a thin, veil-like fabric which is widely available at garden centres and can be bought by the metre. It will provide frost- and wind-chill protection when it gets very cold. I use it during prolonged cold snaps to protect half-hardy plants from getting nuked when temperatures drop below freezing.

Bubble-wrap I sometimes wrap this around the pots to keep the temperature up during cold spells. Some people wrap foliage in it but I'm not keen on that as it doesn't let enough air in.

Sacking A much prettier alternative to the above.

Mulch A layer of leafmould (see page 162) or just ordinary leaves or bark chippings will help to keep roots warm in winter.

Weeds and weeding

Weeds are any plants you don't want in your space. What most of us perceive to be weeds are extremely successful plants that will steal light and moisture from their neighbours, so they have to be eliminated. Some are really simple to get rid of – you just tug at them and they come out easily, roots and all. These are annual weeds, and it's important to remove them before they flower and set seed (although I have to tell you now, that you will never, ever be weed free, not ever, so don't even think of trying to go there, as you will end up a very unhappy person). The trickier weeds are perennial, like dandelions, and these need a bit more cunning.

The best way to control weeds is to learn to recognise them (see Good reading, page 263) and then remove them, either with your own fair hands or with a hoe or trowel. If you are lazy, as I am, make sure you mulch (see page 227), or let them grow and enjoy them – they are still plants, and some are very beautiful indeed.

TACKLING
PERENNIAL WEEDS

The best way to deal with these is persistently to remove their roots. But for some, more drastic action is needed. The most common 'problem weed' is bindweed. If you have an infestation, there's nothing for it but to start from scratch. If the problem is localised to a few areas, though, you can take the following steps.

The first thing to do is work out which bindweed you have, because there are two kinds. *Calystegia sepium* grows to about 2.5m and its roots do not travel down as far as *Convolvulus arvensis*, which has larger flowers and roots that spread horizontally and have been known to reach downwards for 6m. The problem with controlling the latter is that if you pull it, you're likely to break the brittle roots and stimulate more growth, so it's best to do the following.

Get something like a bamboo cane for the plant to climb up and stick it in the ground. You're pretending to be its friend for a while before you strike. Wait until it makes itself at home and starts to twine up the pole – the idea is to get it growing in a controlled area, and not all over your other plants. Next, get a plastic bottle and cut the ends off it, so that you're left with a tube. Put this over the bamboo cane and push it into the soil, so that it surrounds the base of the plant, and remove the cane. Now scrunch the plant down and stuff it into the plastic bottle so that it's all in a tangled heap inside.

When you've done that, go to the nearest petrol station and buy some chocolate. On your way out, get hold of some of those plastic gloves they provide next to each pump. Go home, put the chocolate inside and put on the gloves. Arm yourself with a systemic weedkiller spray (like Glyphosate or Roundup) and nuke your bindweed by spraying carefully inside the plastic tube, with your other gloved hand covering the top so that none of the horrible toxic stuff escapes and lands on your other plants. Make sure all the leaves are completely dripping wet with the spray (you can even get your gloved hand in there and massage it into the foliage to be certain).

Now carefully remove the gloves, putting one inside the plastic tube and the other over the top of it so that it ends up inside out, covering the opening.

Leave the whole thing there, go inside, put the weedkiller away somewhere safe, wash your hands thoroughly and eat the chocolate bar (smiling smugly).

The weedkiller will be absorbed into the plant and kill it from the inside. As long as you've sprayed carefully, no other plants will be affected, and after a week or so you'll be able to remove the plastic and dispose of it. You'll know when to do this because you'll see that the bindweed has died. Be patient, you may need to spray more than once.

If you've got a serious bindweed problem, you may have to start over by clearing the ground and using a total weedkiller, which will render the whole area inactive for some time (and is therefore to be avoided). Alternatively, if practicable, remove all the soil and replace it.

If you don't want to use chemicals, as long as you are fastidious about removing bindweed and other perennial weeds as soon as they appear you'll have control, and the environment will thank you for it. There are also various organic weedkillers available, most of which are based on fatty acids, and these are great for sorting out a small number of less invasive weeds – experiment.

Things that go wrong

Plants can't talk, so the best we can do is to make an educated guess as to why a plant isn't 'performing' as we would like it to. In my experience, working with plants in these situations is part of the joy of growing things — an opportunity to learn. There is nothing more satisfying than bringing something lacklustre back to its full glory, and often the answer is far simpler than we think. It would be futile to attempt a list of possible ailments here; quite apart from filling several large books, it would put you off even beginning this adventure. So, at the risk of sounding like a broken record, I will offer the following:

Find out where your plant comes from.
Use your common sense.

Say, for example, your plant is wilting, the leaves are all floppy and crinkled, and the soil around it is dry: I expect some water wouldn't go amiss here. On the other hand, the soil may be really soggy, in which case your instinct will tell you to let it dry out a bit. Perhaps your plant has yellow leaves, which eventually start falling off; given that it needs light to photosynthesise, it will probably be much happier if you move it somewhere less gloomy. Or you might find that your plant's leaves are all brown and crispy, in which case it's probably been scorched by too much sun.

As you can see, there are many variables, but if you keep going back to that holy trinity of Water, Light and Nutrients, and you've found out the conditions your plant enjoys in its natural habitat and supplied these, you can be pretty sure that if it's still unhappy, the most likely cause will be some sort of pest or disease (see pages 239–44).

Pests

If you are faced with something that is harming your plant, have a good look, find out what's doing the damage and take appropriate action, whatever that may be. But I want to stress that getting hung up on eliminating these sorts of things can be pretty counter-productive, and stop you enjoying your green space. The important thing here is to maintain a balanced attitude. So if you see that a plant is absolutely infested by greenfly, that is something to take action over, but I doubt that you have the time or inclination to go round obsessively checking each and every leaf for sap-suckers.

The way I deal with these things is to amalgamate my bug control with enjoying my garden, which means that if as I sniff my roses of an evening and catch sight of an aphid, I squish it there and then. As a result of this relatively lax attitude, some of the plants necessarily suffer, but there is a payoff, because I also get other wildlife, who like to feed on my pests – and I regard that as more important and interesting than growing 'perfect' plants.

Here are some common pests, and methods of controlling them.

GREENFLY AND BLACKFLY
It's heartbreaking to watch new shoots getting nuked by horrible bugs, and sometimes drastic action is called for. Here is what I use and when:

Organic pesticide Pesticides made from fatty acids and citrus fruits (amongst other things) are now pretty widely available in the shops and online under various brand names. They can be used on edible things and you won't get poisoned. Always read the label.

Provado ultimate bug killer For when desperate times call for desperate measures. This is really noxious stuff, so use it with the utmost care and as little as possible (it kills all the good bugs too), and always spray on a calm day.

Other options:
Try to encourage ladybirds, lacewings and hoverflies Learn to recognise their larvae, which eat up lots of aphids (see Good reading, page 263). You can buy ladybirds by mail order and make houses for them to keep them comfy.

Good husbandry If you keep squishing sap-suckers before they become a problem, this is the best method of control.

WHITEFLY AND OTHER INDOOR FLYING THINGS
I control whitefly by hanging up bright yellow sticky strips, which you can buy at garden centres – the flies can't resist the colour and get stuck on the strip. It's rather darkly satisfying to see more and more of them stuck there over the weeks. They're great for hanging above tomatoes and other whitefly-attracting crops that you may be growing indoors. They will also catch fruit flies, which, although harmless, are not what everyone wants in their kitchen.

Slug wars

You have to be really Zen to subscribe to the idea that a slug is no less entitled to a happy life than you or I. I can get pretty laid back, but I'm not quite there yet. There are lots and lots of ingenious ways to deter or kill slugs and snails. The three methods below are safe, cheap, inconspicuous and not harmful to the environment or other animals (including humans).

Slug trap Make a shallow bowl out of the bottom of a plastic bottle, bury it in the ground and fill it with beer. The slugs will drown in it.
Gritty barriers Slugs like nice smooth wet surfaces to slime all over. They won't cross anything like broken seashells or coarse sand or grit, so put a circle of it around anything precious.
Vaseline Slugs won't cross a thick layer of Vaseline, so apply it around any pots to stop them getting in.

Slugs come out at night, so if you have a really bad problem, go out in dressing gown and wellies with a torch and get them. What you do with them is entirely up to you, but if you want to kill them, salt or secateurs are the two methods most commonly used. Throwing them into other gardens is bad form and they will come back eventually, so don't. Personally I find that small children love nothing better than to be given a jar of slugs.

Protection from small creatures

Birds, squirrels and other small creatures often attack plants in a manner which can only be described as malicious – or at least that's how it feels. I have often woken up to find stems simply chewed through, or small plants unearthed for no apparent reason. I remember once being utterly scandalised to find that a bowl of perfect, blue-bloomed plums I had put on my table had been pilfered (yes, they came inside my house). I found the plums sometime later, half-eaten, buried inside a pot of something equally precious.

These experiences can drive you to distraction if you don't take measures against them, particularly if your space is small and everything in it important to you. Here are some ways in which I protect my plants and thus avoid being sectioned.

Netting You can get this in any old DIY store and it's a great temporary measure. Birds can't get in through it, and squirrels can't bite through it, so although it's unwieldy and ugly, I still use it, particularly for plants at the tender stages of growth.

Cloches These come in many forms and are also used to protect plants from cold and wind. You can get clear plastic cloches that look almost decent but I use cloches made from bamboo, which both look nice and fit neatly around pots.

Tabasco To be honest, I don't know whether this works for sure – all I know is that I have doused it liberally around the stems of precious climbers in pots and they have remained untouched. There is also something nastily amusing about the thought of a squirrel dealing with Tabascoed paws.

Inaccessibility There's not much you can do about birds, and squirrels are like little SAS men: they really will find a way to get pretty much anywhere. What they cannot do, however, is get up the face of a wall when there's nothing for them to hang on to, so if you garden high up, keep the walls around your space clear of vines, or anything they might climb up.

Wire drawers If you're only going to protect osne thing, always, always, always protect your seedlings. Once they're outside in their small pots waiting to be put somewhere it takes only one curious bird to land on top of them and they're done for, which is seriously unhappy-making. I've fashioned a kind of cage out of two wire drawers, one on top of the other, which lets light and air in and keeps other things out. Proper gardeners use cold frames, which are good as well, and which you can close at night to keep out the cold.

Feeding Providing something easier to get at and much more delicious is another option, so bird feeders and similar things make sense – and of course they have the added bonus that you can discover the joys of twitching.

AND SOME THINGS OTHERS DO

Traps, poison, airguns (for squirrels) I won't say I haven't been tempted in my heartbroken, angry moments, but all in all, I'm not into that. Nevertheless, others are, so get advice and keep it legal.

Diseases

Where diseases are concerned I get a bit more active when it comes to dealing with them. Diseases are usually caused by viruses, bacteria or fungi (fungi being the most common – the spores are in the air all around us). The symptoms they produce are usually very visible either on a part of the plant or all over it. If you are buying special plants for an area, it would be well worth seeking out disease-resistant cultivars, which are being developed all the time. As you will see from the methods of control for the following common diseases, the best thing is simply to keep things clean and tidy (see Husbandry on page 231).

ROSE BLACKSPOT — Black splodges appear on the leaves of your roses. The leaf goes yellow, and eventually drops off the plant. This is caused by a fungus. You need to watch for it and remove any leaves promptly and burn them, or prune out infected stems. You can also use a fungicidal spray, though you may need to do this over and over again.

POWDERY MILDEW — A white powder appears on the surface of leaves (see opposite), and sometimes the plant will become distorted. In bad cases the leaves will fall off, and the plant may die. It is caused by fungi, and is usually the result of the plant not getting enough water at its roots, and humidity around the foliage of the plant. Remove any infected leaves, and you can spray it with fungicide, but by far the best thing is to prevent it happening by keeping your plants watered and making sure the airflow around the leaves is maintained. This may be as simple as moving your plant to a different area, or moving something else to create a draught.

RUST — Orange, yellow or brown discoloration of the foliage and stems is actually collections of spores caused by various fungi. It is usually the result of dampness and humidity in the air, which the spores love. Remove infected areas and increase the airflow around the plant (see above).

CHILL OUT — The fundamental point here is that our gardens and green spaces are essentially unnatural environments, and that the problems we encounter as gardeners are most often the result of this fact. Nature finds its own balance, which is why in truly wild places everything that grows is generally healthy. Every plant living there has competed for its place and won. Our gardens are places for the things we want to grow, not for things that necessarily want to grow there – and the sooner you get that, the more philosophical you'll become about the frustrating business of pests, diseases and death.

The Lust List

This book is really one big lust list – the plants in all the recipes belong on it. I've made a lot of friends in the short time I've been learning about plants, and some have huge gardens, and some no garden at all; but what we all have in common is an ever-expanding list of personal favourites that we add to every time we visit a garden or a nursery, or see something fabulous in a magazine – a list of the sort of plants you see, lick your lips greedily and think 'you will be mine'.

My lust list has thus far taken the form of hastily scribbled plant names with double underlining and loads of asterisks and exclamation marks in my notebooks. The only requirement they must fulfil to gain entry to the list is that I should want them very much. For this reason the list is in part a bit of fantasy. There are many plants there that I may never have, but plenty of others that I will. Every virgin gardener should have a lust list. Start one now.

Finally, I want to acknowledge plantswoman extraordinaire Rosemary Campbell-Preston, who showed me her list and encouraged me to start mine. Although the concept of making a list of gorgeous plants is as old as the hills, the words 'lust list' came from her.

NAMES, ORIGIN & HABITAT	DESCRIPTION	SOIL & MOISTURE
Adiantum venustum Woodland margins, crevices and streamsides, China, Himalayas	Evergreen fern with quivering fronds on black stalks that spreads by creeping rhizomes – very, very pretty	Moist, well-drained, moderately fertile
Alchemilla mollis **Lady's mantle** Meadows and light woodland, E. Carpathians, Caucasus, Turkey	Deeply beautiful perennial with soft, hairy pale green leaves that catch water in diamond blobs, and sprays of acid-green flowers	Moist, humus-rich – but it's pretty drought tolerant
Ammi majus Scrub, Europe, N. Africa, W. Asia	Beautiful annual with lacy umbels in white	Moist, well-drained, fertile
Anemone × ***hybrida*** **'Honorine Jobert'** Wide-ranging habitats, N. hemisphere	Perennial with creamy white flowers and yellow stamens	Moist and fertile
Astrantia major **subsp.** ***involucrata*** **'Shaggy'** **Hattie's pincushion** Alpine woods and meadows, C. and E. Europe	Perennial with tiny flowers that are surrounded by a ruff of papery bracts (a term used to describe something between a petal and a leaf) with green veiny tips and pinky centres	Moist, fertile, humus-rich
Athamanta turbith Rocky slopes, meadows and scrubland, S.E. Europe	Sensationally beautiful perennial which looks like lace – even the leaves are feathery	Moderately fertile, well-drained
Chaenomeles × ***superba*** **'Knap Hill Scarlet'** **Flowering quince** Mountain woodland; a hybrid, so of garden origin	Deciduous shrub with spreading branches that have scary-looking thorns (very good against a wall to put off burglars) and outrageous blossom that's so bright it's almost kitsch	Moderately fertile, well-drained
Chimonanthus praecox **Wintersweet** Woodland, China	Upright deciduous shrub which looks like nothing special but has a scent that will blow your mind. It has beautiful claw-like, waxy yellow flowers with a central maroon blotch on bare winter stems	Fertile, well-drained
Corydalis flexuosa Woodland and rocky mountain sites, China	Perennial with delicate feathery leaves and brilliant blue flowers	Moderately fertile, humus-rich, well-drained, not too wet

ASPECT	HEIGHT & SPREAD	FLOWERING TIME	NOTES
Partial shade	15cm x indefinite	All-year gorgeousness	Simply the most delicate hardy evergreen fern around – put it absolutely everywhere
Sun or partial shade	60cm x 75cm	Early summer to early autumn	The leaves are lovely in salads, and if you collect the dew off them in May (alone, naked and by moonlight, of course) it is said to have rather good anti-ageing properties
Full sun or partial shade	30–90cm x 30cm	Summer	Lovely stuff for cutting and adding to other flowers or displaying on its own
Sun or partial shade	1.2m x 1.5m	August to October	Simple and pretty, and comes back and back, spreading itself around. You can get it in pink too
Sun or partial shade	30–90cm x 45cm	Early to mid-summer	Ridiculously photogenic; I seem to have more photos of this flower than any other – I see it and can't resist. The flower dries very well, because of those bracts
Full sun	50cm x 30cm	Summer	Grow lots and lots of this because it makes friends with anything you care to dump it in a vase with
Sun or partial shade	1.5m x 2m	Spring and summer	Comes in lots of colours, all delightful. Keep it trained, as the spines are lethal
Full sun or partial shade	4m x 3m	November to February	May take a while to establish and flower for you but it's worth the wait. Train it against a wall. One stem in a vase will scent your home for a week
Partial shade	30cm x 20cm	April to July	The greek *korydalis* means 'crested lark'. The flowers are manifold and quivering, and true, true blue

NAMES, ORIGIN & HABITAT	DESCRIPTION	SOIL & MOISTURE
Crambe cordifolia Rocky mountain slopes, coastal sites and open grassland, Caucasus	Amazing perennial that shoots up to produce a mass of white flowers. Looks like a huge cloud – and then dies back as quickly as it appears. Very striking	Deep, fertile, well-drained, though will tolerate poor soil
Crinum* × *powellii 'Album' Streamsides and lake margins. This is a hybrid, but its parents hail from South Africa	Utterly beautiful bulbous perennial amaryllis that's been cultivated for the garden. Bears big white lily flowers with lovely scent	Deep, fertile, moist but well-drained, or JI No. 2 in a pot
Daphne bholua **'Jacqueline Postill'** Mountains, E. Himalayas	Evergreen shrub with exquisitely fragrant pink flowers in the dead of winter	Moderately fertile, well-drained but not dry
Dicentra spectabilis **'Alba'** **Lady in the bath** Woodland, Siberia, N. China, Korea	Wonderful, glorious thing that sends up sprays of pure white heart-shaped blobs on long stems. It's a perennial and a real cottage garden favourite, and (hurrah) it comes in pink too!	Moist, fertile, humus-rich
Echinacea **Coneflower** Prairies and gravelly hillsides, C. and E. North America	The ultimate prairie plant, which gives late summer colour – there are loads of varieties to choose from	Deep, well-drained, humus-rich
Erythronium californicum **'White Beauty'** **Dog's-tooth violet** Woodland and meadows, Europe, Asia and N. America	Perennials with veiny or mottled leaves and curled-up pendent flowers	Likes deep, fertile, humus-rich, well-drained soil that never dries out
Eschscholzia californica **California poppy** Grassy, open areas, W. North America	Annual with feathery fern-like foliage and simple, poppy flowers in the most glorious orange	Poor, well-drained
Euphorbia mellifera **Honey spurge** Range of habitats, Madeira	Evergreen shrub and my favourite euphorbia because of the intoxicating scent, but there are many to choose from and they're ideal for a vase	Well-drained, light
Fritillaria meleagris **Snakeshead fritillary** Woodland and open meadows, China	A bulbous perennial of great, great beauty. It has tessellated purple flowers. Also available in white	Fertile, well-drained, or JI No. 2 in a pot

ASPECT	HEIGHT & SPREAD	FLOWERING TIME	NOTES
Full sun, will tolerate partial shade	2.5m x 1.5m	Late spring to mid-summer	A really gratifying plant that everyone always asks about. My mother cuts it and puts it in vases with peonies – cooler than gypsophila
Full sun, and it's borderline hardy, so treat it nicely	1.5m x 30cm	June to August	You have to have space for this plant, as it doesn't look like much when it's not flowering – but it's so worth it when it is. You can keep it outside in all but the coldest areas
Sun or partial shade	2–4m x 1.5m	January/February	Naughty mortal Leucippus disguised himself as a nymph to be near Daphne, but he carelessly showed his bits whilst having a bath and all the nymphs tore him to pieces. Apollo then ran after Daphne who was changed into a tree
Partial shade, though tolerant of full sun as long as the soil is moist	1.2m x 45cm	May to July	If you pick a flower of this and turn it upside down, hold the little wings gently and pull them apart, you will see the lady in her bath
Full sun	60cm or taller	June to October	Echinacea is said to boost the immune system and cure a multitude of ailments – none of which uses has been proven. Its late summer splendour does make you feel pretty good, though
Partial shade	15–35cm x 10cm	March	If you have a moist shady area that you are prepared to leave alone, these beautiful things will slowly increase. It's a waiting game …
Full sun	30cm x 15cm	June to August	Nobody can pronounce this name – but nobody. Raise it from seed
Full sun	2m x 2.5m if it's sheltered and likes you	May	Other beautiful euphorbias are *E. amygdaloides* var. *robbiae*, *E. characias* subsp *wulfenii* and *E. griffithii* 'Fireglow'. Be careful with the sap – it irritates the skin, so wear gloves
Full sun	30cm	March	I grow them in pots because they're precious (and I don't have a meadow). Plant them deep

NAMES, ORIGIN & HABITAT	DESCRIPTION	SOIL & MOISTURE
Galanthus 'Magnet' **Snowdrop** Woodland and rocky areas, Europe to W. Asia	Snowdrops are bulbous perennials. There are lots of different ones, but this one is big and simple and pure. I love it	Moist, but well-drained soil that does not dry out in summer
Geranium phaeum **Dusky cranesbill** Mountainous regions	Herbaceous perennial with deep purple to white flowers	Most soils, moist but not waterlogged
Gloriosa superba 'Rothschildiana' **Glory lily** Woodland, riverbanks, Africa, India	A real 'I want one of those' plant. This is a tuberous perennial climber that really lives up to its name. The flowers look like flames	Fertile, well-drained soil outdoors, or a pot of JI No. 2
Helenium 'Moerheim Beauty' Swampy meadows and woodland margins, North and Central America	Sumptuous burnt orange perennial for late-summer beauty. There are many, many different permutations	Fertile, moist but well-drained
Hosta 'Hadspen Blue' **Plantain lily** Rocky streamsides, woodland, China, Korea, Japan	All hostas are lush things and brilliant to have in a pot. They are perennials and grown primarily for their exquisite leaves. There are lots of different ones to choose from. They like shade, so are perfect for dark corners	Fertile, moist, well-drained
Ipomoea tricolor **Morning glory** Diverse habitats, tropical Central and South America	Really fast-growing twining annual that's easy to grow from seed with hypnotic blue trumpet flowers (get 'Heavenly Blue')	Moderately fertile, well drained, or JI No. 2 in a pot
Iris confusa China	A crested iris with evergreen leaves that throws up flower stems with masses of successional white flowers with yellow crests	Moist, humus-rich, or JI No. 2 in a pot with added grit
Iris germanica var. *florentina* **Orris root** Mediterranean	Rhizomatous, bearded iris with evergreen leaves (usually) and big, white, beautifully scented flowers	Well-drained, fertile, neutral to slightly acid, or JI No. 2 in a pot with added grit
Iris sibirica C. and E. Europe, Turkey, Russia	Rhizomatous, beardless Siberian iris with thin leaves and violet blue flowers	Moist, well-drained, neutral to slightly acid

ASPECT	HEIGHT & SPREAD	FLOWERING TIME	NOTES
Partial shade	20cm x 8cm	February, March	Galanthophilia is a cult – and a very good one at that. Check out G. 'S. Arnott' for its scent
Sun or shade	80cm x 45cm	Spring to summer	My favourite geranium – bowed head and sultry colour. Comes in white too
Full sun in a sheltered spot	2m x 30cm	Summer to autumn	These flowers are flown in from Africa for the cut flower market, each in its own blown-up plastic bag. That's reason enough to grow one yourself
Full sun	90cm x 60cm	Summer to autumn	Fabulous for cutting
Full or partial shade	25cm x 60cm	Hostas start unfurling (beautifully) in spring and throw up their flowers in summer	Slugs and snails really adore eating hostas, so protect your pots with a thick line of Vaseline around the base and rim of the pot – unless, that is, you like holey hostas, which can be uniquely beautiful
Full sun	3–4m high	June to August	The Aztecs used the seeds as a hallucinogen, but just looking at a flower is enough for me
Full sun or partial shade	1m or more	April	Loads of flowers on bamboo-like stems. Reminds me more of an orchid than an iris
Full sun	60–120cm	May	Used as a base note in perfumery, and a constituent of Bombay Sapphire, amongst other things, this is an incredibly obliging iris and the smell is off the scale
Full sun or partial shade	50–120cm	Early summer	Loves being next to a pond or somewhere like it, but this is not essential – just make sure you plant lots

NAMES, ORIGIN & HABITAT	DESCRIPTION	SOIL & MOISTURE
Lathyrus latifolius **Everlasting pea** Open woodland, shingle banks and wasteland, S. Europe	Perennial climber, so you can get your pea fix even if you forget the sweet peas	Fertile, humus-rich, well-drained
Lonicera × *purpusii* **'Winter Beauty'** **Winter-flowering honeysuckle** Woodlands and thickets, N. hemisphere	Deciduous or semi-evergreen shrub that will rock your world in winter because the scent is sublime	Well-drained, or JI No. 3 in a pot
Lunaria annua **Honesty** Disturbed ground and uncultivated fields, Europe	Annual or biennial, with lovely purple flowers and moon-shaped seedheads	Pretty much anything will do
Mathiasella bupleuroides **'Green Dream'** Mexico	Extraordinary and beautiful perennial plant only recently discovered, with green flowers	Well-drained, moist, or JI No. 2 in a pot
Narcissus bulbocodium France, Portugal, Spain and N. Africa	A small daffodil with a hoop petticoat rather than kick pleats	Moist, well-drained, moderately fertile, neutral to acid
Osmanthus delavayi Woodland, W. China	Evergreen shrub with arching branches	Fertile, well-drained soil
Paeonia lactiflora **'Sarah Bernhardt'** Meadows, scrub and rocky places in Europe, Asia and North America	Gorgeous, clump-forming herbaceous perennial with massive cabbagey blooms	Deep, fertile, moist, well-drained
Papaver bracteatum Wide-ranging habitats, N. Iran	Lovely bristly perennial poppy with bloody petals and a black blotch	Fertile, well-drained
Papaver somniferum **Opium poppy** Wide-ranging habitats, Unknown origin	Annual with bowl-shaped flowers in a wide range of colours from white to deep red and awesome seed pods	Fertile, well-drained

ASPECT	HEIGHT & SPREAD	FLOWERING TIME	NOTES
Full sun or light dappled shade	2m high	Summer to early autumn	Sadly no scent, but gorgeous pinky purple flowers that come back every year
Full sun or partial shade	2m x 2.5m	Late winter, early spring	This shrub has arching stems, making it a perfect candidate for training against a wall. If you are a winter-phobic, this will get you out
Full sun or partial shade	90cm x 30cm	Spring to summer	Beloved by bees and butterflies, and the papery seedheads are great for decoration
Full sun	1m x 50cm	Summer	Possibly the trendiest plant on the planet right now, though I have a feeling it'll still be lustworthy for years to come. Named after a plant-hunter called Mildred
Full sun or dappled shade	10–15cm	Mid-spring	Demure and pretty, and particularly good en masse. You need to leave the flowers on until the seeds have dispersed
Sun or partial shade	2–6m x 4m	April, May	This is a great thing to use for hedging and topiary, or to train against a wall. There's a smaller-leaved version called *Osmanthus × burkwoodii*
Full sun or partial shade	90cm x 90cm	May, June, July	'There are five kinds of actresses,' said Mark Twain: 'bad actresses, fair actresses, good actresses, great actresses . . . and then there is Sarah Bernhardt.'
Full sun	1.2m x 90cm	Early summer	Very similar to *P. orientale*, except it's taller and stiffer — and of course it comes back every year
Full sun	1m x 30cm	Summer	The seed pod of this plant is used for all sorts of things, some more useful than others. Poppy seeds are delicious and completely safe to eat from your own plants

NAMES, ORIGIN & HABITAT	DESCRIPTION	SOIL & MOISTURE
Passiflora **Passion flower** Tropical woodland, C. and W. South America	Evergreen climber with weird, complicated, amazing flowers. It's half-hardy but seems to survive being outside all year on my balcony, where it clothes the railings. This one is called 'Amethyst'	Moderately fertile, moist but well-drained, or JI No 3. in a container
Philadelphus coronarius **'Variegatus'** **Mock orange** Scrub and rocky hillsides, S. Europe, Caucasus	Deciduous shrub with deliciously smelly, creamy flowers and variegated leaves	Moderately fertile, well-drained
Pittosporum tobira **Japanese mock orange** Wide-ranging habitats, China	Beautiful evergreen shrub with big dark green leathery leaves and creamy flowers that smell like gardenias	Fertile, moist but well-drained, or JI No. 3 in a pot
Polygonatum odoratum **Solomon's seal** Woodland, Europe, Caucasus, Russia, Japan	Exquisite rhizomatous perennial with arching stems and rows of leaves and pendent fragrant white flowers with green tips – very restrained and chic	Fertile, humus-rich, moist but well-drained
Pulsatilla vulgaris **var.** *rubra* **Pasque flower** Short turf and alpine meadows, W. France to Ukraine	Deciduous perennial with feathery leaves and bell-shaped, silky hairy flowers from deep purple to white	Fertile, very well-drained
Rosa banksiae W. and C. China	A species rose which smothers whatever it touches with white flowers that are violet scented	Moderately fertile, moist but well-drained
Rosa **'Madame Alfred Carrière'** Asia, Europe, N. Africa and North America	Evergreen perennial climber with gorgeous, cabbagey, fabulously scented blooms, pale pink to white	Moderately fertile, humus-rich, moist but well-drained
Rosa **'New Dawn'** Modern climbers begin with 'New Dawn'. It appeared as a sport of another rose	Glorious pale pink/white vigorous climbing rose that flowers continually and is beautifully, romantically scented	Moderately fertile, moist but well-drained
Rudbeckia hirta **Coneflower, black-eyed Susan** Moist meadows and light woodland, North America	Annual rudbeckias give wonderful reliable colour all summer, and are great for cut flowers. This one is called 'Cherokee Sunset'	Moderately fertile, well-drained soil that does not dry out

ASPECT	HEIGHT & SPREAD	FLOWERING TIME	NOTES
Full sun or partial shade	10m high	Summer to autumn	Symbolic of the passion – 10 petals for the faithful apostles, 72 filaments for the crown of thorns, 3 stigmas for the nails
Full sun or partial shade	2.5m x 2m	Early summer	Especially for virgins – also try to seek out P. 'Virginal', which has flowers that are double, very fragrant and to be worshipped
Full sun or partial shade; not fully hardy so needs shelter	1.5m x 3m	Early summer	There's a smaller one called 'Nanum', which makes a perfect mound in a pot. This stuff is lovely as informal, sexy hedging
Full sun or partial shade	85cm x 30cm	Late spring, early summer	This plant has been used medicinally for centuries, for everything from period pain to broken bones. Best planted en masse
Full sun	10–20cm x 20cm	Spring	Named for its Easter flowering time. Loads of feel appeal
Full sun, sheltered wall	12m x 6m	Summer to autumn	Named for Lady Banks, wife of botanist Sir Joseph. There are single and double varieties – both smell of violets though, so you can have either
Will tolerate some shade and likes a bit of shelter	5m x 3m	June to November, but if it likes you it'll flower all year	The first rose I fell in love with
Tolerates partial shade	3m x 2.5m	June to November, depending on where you are	Awarded the title 'World's Favourite Rose' in 1997, this was the first plant ever to be patented (US Patent No. 1, 1930)
Full sun or partial shade	30–90cm x 30–45cm	Summer to autumn	These will self-seed if you let them. Best planted in huge drifts for maximum impact

NAMES, ORIGIN & HABITAT	DESCRIPTION	SOIL & MOISTURE

Sarcococca confusa
Christmas box
Forest and thickets in China,
the Himalayas and S.E. Asia

The ultimate evergreen shrub. Thrives on
neglect and provides strong sweet scent in
winter when all is gloomy

Fertile,
well-drained

Solanum crispum
Chilean potato tree
Wide range of habitats,
Peru and Chile

If you've ever seen a potato in flower you'll
recognise that this plant is from the same
family. It's an evergreen or semi-evergreen
scrambler with purple flowers

Moderately
fertile, moist but
well-drained, or
JI No. 2 in a pot

Tellima grandiflora
Fringe cups
Moist woodland,
North America

Delightful herbaceous perennial with little
white bell-flowers with fringed petals

Moist, humus-
rich, but will
tolerate dry
conditions

Trachelospermum jasminoides
Woodland,
China, Korea, Japan

Evergreen twining climber with deliciously
scented salverform white flowers

Fertile,
well-drained,
or JI No. 3

Tricyrtis formosana
Toad lily
Moist woodland,
mountains and cliffs,
Taiwan

Rhizomatous perennial with weird and
wonderful spotty fleshy flowers and big
fat stigmas

Moist but
well-drained,
humus-rich

Verbena bonariensis
Prairies, wasteland
and hillsides,
South America

Perennial with purple flowers on tall
stiff stems

Moist,
well-drained,
moderately
fertile, or
JI No. 2 in a pot

Viburnum × bodnantense
'Dawn'
Hybrid between *V. farreri* and
V. grandiflorum, both native
to woodland in China

Deciduous shrub with dark green leaves and
headily scented rosy pink flowers borne on
bare wood for ages

Moderately
fertile, moist but
well-drained

Vitis coignetiae
Grape vine
Woodland and thickets,
Korea and Japan

Woody deciduous climber with massive
leathery, veiny heart-shaped leaves that blush
bright red in autumn. If you want edible
grapes, choose *Vitis* 'Brant'

Well-drained,
humus-rich

Wisteria
Moist woodland,
China, Korea, Japan and
C. and S. USA

Woody deciduous climbers with pendent
pea-like scented flowers in colours from
white to deep purple

Fertile, moist,
well-drained

ASPECT	HEIGHT & SPREAD	FLOWERING TIME	NOTES
Deep or partial shade	2m x 1m	Winter	One or two twigs brought indoors will scent the whole house for days
Full sun	Up to 6m high	Summer	Also available in white. Perfect for railings or a trellis or arbour
Partial shade	40cm x 25cm	Late spring to mid-summer	Lovely semi-evergreen thing that rewards the eyes and nose for being granted a closer look, and good for difficult areas of dry shade
Full sun or partial shade	9m high	Summer	Brilliant for clothing a wall and surrounding yourself with heady scent in summer
Deep or partial shade	80cm x 45cm	Early autumn	You need to have these where you can see them. They look like orchids or as if they were something only an 'expert' would be able to grow. They will, in short, impress your friends
Full sun	2m x 45cm	Mid-summer to early autumn	Perfect for creating a transparent screen, and delicious to bees
Full sun or partial shade	3m x 2m	Late autumn through to spring	Other viburnums I love are *V. tinus*, *V. carlesii* and *V. opulus*. All tough, beautiful plants
Full sun or partial shade	15m high	The flowers are insignificant, but the leaves are beautiful throughout the growing season, particularly in autumn, when they go nuts	When you buy this, do so when it has some leaves, as the plants are variable amd sometimes they lack the bumpy, leathery quality that makes this plant so gorgeous. The leaves are huge – perfect for table mats at Hallowe'en
Full sun or partial shade	9m high	Spring to summer	The two wisterias most commonly grown are *W. floribunda* (Japanese) and *W. sinensis* (Chinese). If you want something utterly spectacular, choose *W. floribunda* 'Multijuga', whose racemes of flowers can grow over a metre long

Suppliers

The following are all nurseries or websites I have visited and bought from and that I keep going back to, but the list is certainly not exhaustive. You can phone up the majority of these places and get a real expert on the other end of the line who will be more than happy to help you with whatever you need to know.

GARDEN CENTRES

B&Q: www.diy.com; **Wyevale**: www.wyevale.co.uk; **Homebase**: www.homebase.co.uk

BRILLIANT SMALL NURSERIES

Cotswold Garden Flowers
Sands Lane, Badsey, Worcestershire, WR11 7EZ
Tel: 01386 833 849

Phoenix Perennial Plants
Paice Lane, Medstead, Alton, Hampshire, GU34 5PR
Tel: 01420 560 695

Spinners Garden and Rare Plant Nursery
School Lane, nr Lymington, Hampshire, SO41 5QE
Tel: 01590 673 347

SPECIALIST NURSERIES

Alpines www.darcyeverest.co.uk
Aquatics www.lilieswatergardens.co.uk
Bulbs www.avonbulbs.com, www.broadleighbulbs.co.uk
Carnivorous www.littleshopofhorrors.co.uk
Cyclamen www.tilebarn-cyclamen.co.uk
Ferns www.fibrex.co.uk
Fruit www.crown-nursery.co.uk, www.blackmoor.co.uk
Garlic www.reallygarlicky.co.uk
Ivy www.fibrex.co.uk
Lavender www.downderry-nursery.co.uk
Pelargoniums www.firtreespelargoniums.co.uk
Roses www.davidaustinroses.com, www.classicroses.co.uk
Seeds www.specialplants.net, www.thompson-morgan.com, www.suttons.co.uk, www.dobies.co.uk, www.fothergills.co.uk
Trees for presents www.tree2mydoor.com
Violets www.grovenurseries.co.uk

OTHER STUFF

Root trainers www.rootrainers.co.uk
Secure plant hangers Email christon1266@aol.com
Great places for plants and all things gardening
www.burncoose.co.uk, www.crocus.co.uk, www.sarahraven.com, www.capitalgardens.co.uk, www.daylesfordorganic.com, www.clifton.co.uk, www.petershamnurseries.com, www.gardenseeker.com.

Good reading

I have a huge number of gardening books, but these are the ones I find myself referring to again and again, along with the magazines I subscribe to. (I have starred my favourites.)

PRACTICAL   **The Botanical Garden: Perennials and Annuals** Volume 2 by Roger Phillips and Martyn Rix (Macmillan, 2002)
Collins Tree Guide by Owen Johnson (Collins, 2006)
Expert series by D.G. Hessayon (Expert) ❊
Field Guide to the Wild Flowers of Britain (Reader's Digest, 2001)
Grow Your Own Vegetables by Joy Larkcom (Frances Lincoln, 2002)
Hillier Manual of Trees and Shrubs by Hillier Nurseries (David & Charles, 1998) ❊
Introductory Plant Biology by Kingsley R. Stern, James Bidlack and Shelley Jansky (McGraw-Hill, 2007) ❊
Jekka's Complete Herb Book by Jekka McVicar (Kyle Cathie, 2007)
RHS A–Z Encyclopedia of Garden Plants by Christopher Brickell (Dorling Kindersley, 2003) ❊
RHS Pests and Diseases by Pippa Greenwood and Andrew Halstead (Dorling Kindersley, 2007) ❊
RHS Plant Finder (Dorling Kindersley, annual publication) ❊
RHS Propagating Plants by Alan R. Toogood (Dorling Kindersley, 2006) ❊
Wild Flowers (Collins Nature Guides) by Wolfgang Lippert and D. Podleich (Collins, 1994)
The Yellow Book: NGS Gardens Open for Charity (National Gardens Scheme, annual publication)

PLEASURE   **A Gentle Plea for Chaos** by Mirabel Osler (Bloomsbury, 2000)
The Education of a Gardener by Russell Page (Harvill Press, 1995)
In Your Garden Again by Vita Sackville-West (Frances Lincoln, 2004)
The Making of a Garden by Rosemary Verey (Frances Lincoln, 2001)
Vista: The Culture and Politics of Gardens by Noel Kingsbury and Tim Richardson (Frances Lincoln, 2005)
We Made a Garden by Margery Fish (B.T. Batsford, 2002)

MAGAZINES   **Gardeners' World Magazine**
The Garden
The Plantsman
Which? Gardening

Index

Abyssinian banana (*Ensete ventricosum*) 217
Acer palmatum (Japanese maple) 74
Achillea seedheads 57
acid-loving plants 21, 228
Acidanthera 213
Adiantum venustum 248–9
adzuki beans 94
Alchemilla mollis (lady's mantle) 179, 248–9
alfalfa seeds 94
Allegheny monkey musk (*Mimulus ringens*) 205
Allium
  A. christophii seedheads 57
  A. sativum (garlic) 114–15
  A. schoenoprasum (chives) 85, 86
  A. schubertii seedheads 57
almonds 94
Aloe vera 55
Aloysia triphylla (lemon verbena) 128
alpine plants 13, 72, 74
amaryllis bulbs 182
amelanchier blossom 164
Ammi majus 248–9
Anemone × *hybrida* 'Honorine Jobert' 248–9
Anethum graveolens (dill) 87
annuals 12, 60
Anthriscus cerefolium (chervil) 87
aphids 170
apple mint (*Mentha suaveolens*) 82
aquatic plants 13, 205, 207
asparagus 120
Asplenium scolopendrium (hart's tongue fern) 37
Astrantia major subsp. *involucrata* 'Shaggy' (Hattie's pincushion) 248–9
Athamanta turbith 248–9

bagna cauda 136
banana, Abyssinian (*Ensete ventricosum*) 217
barrenwort (*Epimedium*) 198
basil (*Ocimum basilicum*) 88–9
baskets
  hanging (with strawberries) 102–3
  spring bulbs in 157
bay (*Laurus nobilis*) 86
beans
  broad 113
  mung 93–4
  runner 118
bedding plants 60–61
bergamot (*Monarda didyma*) 82
biennials 13
bindweed 236
birds 243
black-eyed Susan (*Rudbeckia hirta*) 256–7
blackfly 113, 239
blackspot, rose 170, 244
blossom, indoor 164–5
blueberries 110, 112
  blueberry muffins 112
borage (*Borago officinalis*) 91, 134

broad beans (*Vicia faba*) 113
bromeliads 13, 210
bulbous plants 13
bulbs, spring (in baskets) 157
burnet (*Sanguisorba*) seedheads 57
Butomus umbellatus (flowering rush) 205
butternut squash 75–6
buying plants 15

cacti 13, 21, 38
Calendula (marigold) 61, 91
California poppy (*Eschscholzia californica*) 250–51
Calystegia sepium 236
Capsicum (chillies) 202, 204
carnivorous plants 186, 189
carrots 101
Centaurea cyanus (cornflower) 101
Ceropegia linearis subsp. *woodii* (hearts on a string) 33
Chaenomeles × *superba* 'Knap Hill Scarlet' (flowering quince) 248–9
cherry tree (*Prunus*) blossom 164
chervil (*Anthriscus cerefolium*) 87
chickpeas 94
Chilean potato tree (*Solanum crispum*) 258–9
chillies (*Capsicum*) 202, 204
Chimonanthus praecox (wintersweet) 248–9
chives (*Allium schoenoprasum*) 85, 86
Christmas box (*Sarcococca confusa*) 258–9
Christmas wreaths 78
citrus fruit
  Citrus aurantium/sinensis (orange) 138
  C. limon (lemon) 138–9
  C. reticulata (clementine) 138
clay soil 227–8
clementine (*Citrus reticulata*) 138
climbers 12
cloches 243
cloning 174–5
Cobaea scandens (cup and saucer vine) 209
compost 20–21, 172–3, 226, 227
coneflower (*Echinacea*) 57, 250–51
coneflower (*Rudbeckia hirta*) 256–7
Convolvulus arvensis 236
coriander (*Coriandrum sativum*) 87
Cornelian cherry (*Cornus mas*) 164
cornflower (*Centaurea cyanus*) 101
Cornus mas (Cornelian cherry) 164
Corydalis flexuosa 248–9
crab apple (*Malus*) blossom 164
Crambe cordifolia 250–51
cranesbill, dusky (*Geranium phaeum*) 252–3
Crinum × *powellii* 'Album' 250–51
Crocus sativus (saffron crocus) 117
crystallised petals 29, 146
Cucurbita (squash) 75–6
cut flowers 34, 40, 42, 47
cuttings, taking 158–9
  see also cloning

Acknowledgements

I am indebted to so many people (mostly for putting up with me) during the writing of this book; they have all helped in different ways to bring it to fruition.

For creative input, commitment and hard work in equal measure, I want to thank everyone at Bloomsbury, especially Natalie Hunt who has put this book together with a magical and consistent mix of patience and enthusiasm. Warm thanks also to Lisa Fiske, Ruth Logan, Anya Rosenberg, Anna Robinson, Kate Tindel-Robertson and Anne Askwith. I'd like to thank my agent, Eugenie Furniss who, with Rowan Lawton, made everything so easy and has been a constant source of encouragement.

Thanks too to Jill Mead, whose exquisite photographs have made this book more beautiful than I could ever have dreamed possible, to Friederike Huber, who designed it so perfectly and instinctively, and to Kate Osborn, for her gorgeous illustrations.

For support, friendship and general bright-eyed, kind interest, all of the following have contributed to the writing of this book, and it is a better one for my having known them: Sally Brampton, Rosemary Campbell-Preston, Rose Campher, Adrian Drury, Ruth Field, Fergus Gilroy, Cameron Hill, Natalia Illingworth, Veronique Jackson, Natasha Manley, Elena Mejia, Kathleen McMahon, Dorrie Mcveigh, Tommi Miers, Georgina Oliver, Simon Pyle, Eileen Quinn, Natasha Randall, Jenny and Richard Raworth, Gabrielle Ross, Karen Ross-Smith, Claudia Rothermere, Paula Scully, Rupert Shaw, Grub Smith, James Stockton and Katherine van Tienhoven.

Heartfelt thanks to my parents, Raphael and Marillyn, and my brothers, David and Edmund, who have been there from the beginning, and for Mr Pug, cruelly usurped by the lap-top … my knees are yours again.

And most importantly, to my editor, Katie Bond, who, to my surprise and delight, saw this book sleeping inside me and pulled it, blinking, into the sunshine; ever grateful, I can't say thank you enough.

In memory of my grandmother,
Christian Lewis, with love.

First published in Great Britain 2009

Bloomsbury Publishing Plc, 36 Soho Square, London
W1D 3QY

A CIP catalogue record for this book is available from
the British Library.

ISBN 978 0 7475 9398 0
10 9 8 7 6 5 4 3 2 1

Designer: Friederike Huber
Photographer: Jill Mead
Illustrator: Kate Osborn
Indexer: Vicki Robinson

Printed in Singapore by Tien Wah Press

www.bloomsbury.com